MW00815354

Say So

A heart-to-heart with God in the Psalms

Monty F. Waldron

Copyright © 2014 by Monty F. Waldron

Say So
A heart-to-heart with God in the Psalms
by Monty F. Waldron

Printed in the United States of America

ISBN 9781498415972

All rights reserved solely by the author. The author guarantees all contents are original and do not infringe upon the legal rights of any other person or work. No part of this book may be reproduced in any form without the permission of the author. The views expressed in this book are not necessarily those of the publisher.

Scripture quotations taken from the English Standard Version (ESV). Copyright © 2001 by Crossway, a publishing ministry of Good News Publishers. Used by permission. All rights reserved.

www.xulonpress.com

The word on the street about *Say So* ...

Taking a healthy pause to reflect on our Creator is like balm to a chafed soul. Do yourself a favor and practice a little Psalm soul-care by reading *Say So*; filled with insightful discoveries of a living and loving God.
- **Mark Crull**, Executive Pastor at Northview Church,
Author of *Disciple²*

In a world filled with so much noise, it's so necessary to be still and reflect on the greatness of God. This book is a great companion in our quest to encourage our hearts with God's love.
- **Derek Minor**, Hip Hop artist,
co-founder of *Reflection Music Group*

Do you long for a deeper relationship with God but aren't sure where to begin? Start here and let a seasoned pastor and fellow traveler guide you into the Psalms and closer to the heart of your Heavenly Father. With vulnerability, wisdom, and passion Monty Waldron will help you engage God's Word in a fresh way in these hope-filled pages.
- **Jonathan Morrow**, Speaker & Author of
Questioning the Bible: 11 Major Challenges to the Bible's Authority,
Founder of ThinkChristianly.org

God has revealed so much of Himself in the beauty and raw truth of the Psalms. Struggle, heartache, joy, disappointment, hurt, delight...the human condition in a fallen world pours out of the pens of the God-inspired writers of this book of poetry and worship. The truth-filled chapters of *Say So* consistently shine a light on these inspired words and have challenged, confronted, comforted and encouraged me to explore more deeply my own heart and the heart of my Heavenly Father. I am grateful for my friend, Monty Waldron and for his labor of love in writing this book.
- **Phil Herndon**, co-author of *Voice of the Heart Workbook*

Monty examines the Word of God with the mind of a scholar and a poet. His words about these passages are as approachable as a conversation over coffee–authentic and transparent about the struggles that we share with the authors of these relevant texts that ultimately point to a risen Savior.

–**David Stevenson**, Singer/Songwriter with *Manic Bloom*

Throughout the last 10 years of church planting and church growing, there has been a steady hand of integrity and friendship in my life. His name is Monty Waldron! I am a better Christ follower, pastor, husband, father and friend because God has graced my life and ministry with him. His reflections on the Psalms are simply an extension of the life I've seen first hand. Enjoy!

- **Jeff Patton**, Teaching Pastor at Fellowship Bible Church and FamilyLife *Weekend to Remember* conference speaker

Say So (Vol I)

A heart-to-heart with God in the Psalms

Monty F. Waldron

To Kimberly, my bride, best friend and co-laborer.

You are the Proverbs 31 woman I prayed for decades ago. I treasure the journey we've made since the day we said "I do." Your relentless pursuit of the God of the Psalms and the ease at which those sacred songs leave your lips refreshes my soul and stirs me to love and good deeds.

"You have captivated my heart" – Song of Solomon 4:9

CONTENTS

INTRODUCTION

I**know what it's like to feel alone.** Some of my earliest memories are saturated with fear and sadness around not fitting in. I longed to be known and loved, but wondered if that was truly possible. When it came to God, I assumed things were no different. I believed God existed, but figured He knew what a misfit I was (not to mention a host of sinful shortcomings), and probably didn't want much to do with me.

With childlike simplicity and deep resolve I determined to show God and everyone else that I did belong. Performance was my strategy, achievement my friend. The world rewarded winners with attention and acceptance, so I set out to be the best at whatever I did. I devoted myself to excellence believing that eventually, if I was good enough, loneliness would become a thing of the past.

While I experienced some success along the way, my deepest longing to be known and loved wasn't satisfied. The attention I gained with each accomplishment was short-lived and I was left to prove myself all over again. Performance became a ruthless master, dangling hope in front of me of the intimacy I craved, but never delivering.

During high school I was told the greatest news I've ever heard even to this day. I had gotten it all wrong with God. He did know how short I fell, but that had nothing to do with how He felt about me (and everyone else for that matter). I learned that He loved me not for how well I performed, but for who I was. The mere fact that I existed, that I was created by Him with His imprint on my life, was reason enough for Him to feel great affection for me. What an awesome surprise!

I found that belonging was ultimately about asking God to do for me what I could never do for myself. So I did. In the mountains of Colorado, I asked God to be my father, to forgive me of all my sin and to make me into the man He intended me to be ... a lifelong overhaul from the inside out. My assurance of acceptance was rooted in the fact that He had sent His son, Jesus Christ, to suffer the consequences of my sin so that I could be brought forever into His family.

That moment set me on a journey throughout the endless territory of God's unconditional love. The terrain has been challenging but the path has led me to places of breathtaking beauty and genuine joy. Old habits die hard and I've reverted to seasons of performance and self-reliance along the way. But my heavenly Father has repeatedly taken me back to the reality of His grace (unmerited favor) and the refuge of belonging found only in Him.

That kind of intimacy shows up again and again in the book of Psalms. The biblical collection has been called the hymnbook of God's people in that it contains poetic songs composed in the broad spectrum of human experience. Literally titled the *book of praises*, Psalms consists of heartaches and hopes, longings and losses, fears and faith inspired by the God in whom broken people have placed their trust. In its pages, our Creator reveals His relentless heart for humanity and His infinite capacity to rescue rebels from the destruction of their own devices.

So I invite you to walk with me through this collection of sacred songs. Each chapter offers a glimpse into an honest dialogue between a loving Father and His children. Far from pious platitudes, we're going to encounter unsanitized prayers made to a God who welcomes us into His presence with struggles and celebration alike. With each psalm, we'll find that we're not alone in our struggle to make sense of life in a fallen world, and we'll gain confidence entrusting our hearts to God.

Along the way, I urge you to put pen to the page. I've included my personal thoughts and impressions prompted by each psalm, and I hope you'll do the same in the space provided. This volume includes the first 50 psalms of a total 150 contained in the Old Testament. With 52 weeks in a year, you can read, reflect upon and respond to one psalm per week. This allows time for you to read the psalm over a period of several days and absorb its message before setting out to write. My journal entries are intended to stir your thinking and model the idea of responding in a concrete way to God's initiative.

The words of these ancient children of God aren't meant to merely be observed, they are meant to be engaged. They exist to stir in us a heart-to-heart conversation of our own with God. God knows the sub-stance of your heart, so put it to words ... Say So! Enter into the intimacy of talking openly with your heavenly Father as He speaks to you through the truth of His word.

If you are a Christ-follower, if you have entrusted your life to Christ by grace through faith, then you have three invaluable resources avail-able to you throughout your trek through the Psalms. First of all, you have the Scriptures themselves, inspired and preserved by God Himself through human authors (2 Timothy 3:16-17; 2 Peter 1:21). Second, as a Christian you are indwelt and guided by the Holy Spirit (Ephesians 1:13-14; John 16:13). Finally, you have the community of faith avail-able to you which has engaged and applied the Scriptures for 2000 years (Ephesians 5:18-21; Colossians 3:16). Where you find unity among these three resources – God's word, God's Spirit and God's people – you can have confidence that you have arrived at a reliable understanding of God's voice in your life. *Note: One resource that can come in handy while studying Scripture is a commentary, an interpretive guide helping span the gap between the ancient world and our own. Allen Ross, Derek Kidner and Tremper Longman III have each completed some very helpful and current commentaries on the Psalms.*

If you are not yet a Christ-follower, I have to assume that the fact you are reading this book is reassuring evidence that God is initiating in your life and striving to reveal His great affection for you. I encourage you to listen and consider the possibility that despite anything in your past, God longs to adopt you into His family and cultivate in you the genuine spir-itual life you were created to experience.

Before we embark on this journey, let's get the lay of the land. We're dealing with ancient words written by several different authors in a different language to a different culture. A thoughtful approach to the psalms will enable us to grasp their time-bound meaning and their time-less significance.

As we approach the Psalms, it's helpful to know that each (with a few exceptions) was written independently of the others over hundreds of years. Most emerged as a response to specific life circumstances of the author, i.e. King David wrote Psalm 51 as a repentant confession after adultery with Bathsheba. That being the case, we can expect to resonate with the Psalm's emotional and theological substance while not necessarily having identical experiences as those of their authors.

These spiritual songs are written in the form of Hebrew poetry, so we are wise to keep an eye out for some distinct features. Artistically, there is rhythm and movement not unlike most other poetic expressions. Instances of repetition often signal the focus of an individual psalm. The use of parallelism provides structure for the arrangement of ideas. Phrases are purposefully coupled so as to emphasize or clarify the concept being shared. In addition, vivid imagery is utilized to figuratively describe all manner of subjects. To misinterpret this literary feature is to miss the beauty unique to poetic style.

Amid the creativity, all of the psalms are written with obvious purpose. Though the book of Psalms contains a great deal of variety, there are five general categories that characterize the intent behind the content. The first is *hymns of praise*. These songs highlight the attributes and activities of God for the purpose of provoking worship among the people of God. Another type is called a *lament*. These convey emotions of sadness and fear associated with painful circumstances often resolving with a declaration of praise for God's sufficiency. Next are *psalms of thanksgiving*, declarations of gratitude for various forms of provision made by God in times of need. *Wisdom psalms* are known for guiding the thoughts and actions of God's people to lives of obedience and blessing. Finally, *liturgical psalms* are associated with notable events in the religious practices of Israel which provide conceptual guidance as we think today about approaching God in worship.

The vast majority of psalms have a journal-like quality; heartfelt prayer originally directed to God, but recorded for the benefit of humanity. As a result, they serve not only to inform us, but to model the expansive pathways of talking with God. Each song ushers us into the private world of a child seeking audience with his Father by faith. Praise and pleas for intervention saturate these verses, reminding us that intimacy with God is found in the give and take of conversation. With that in mind, let's walk together into the Psalm's fruitful landscape.

Psalm 1

[1]Blessed is the man who walks not in the counsel of the wicked, nor stands in the way of sinners, nor sits in the seat of scoffers;
[2]but his delight is in the law of the Lord, and on his law he meditates day and night.
[3]He is like a tree planted by streams of water that yields its fruit in its season, and its leaf does not wither. In all that he does, he prospers.
[4]The wicked are not so, but are like chaff that the wind drives away.
[5]Therefore the wicked will not stand in the judgment, nor sinners in the congregation of the righteous;
[6]for the Lord knows the way of the righteous, but the way of the wicked will perish.

Thirsty

Spiritual blessing is the fruit of focus.

We are thirsty-souled people living in a land crowded with so-called wells of wisdom, most of which contain toxic, stagnant opinions tainted by the best of humanity's intellect. Some wells, though, are brimming with life-giving truth that originates with God, not man. It is wisdom man doesn't conceive, but only receives.

Fruitfulness is had by those who choose to drench their souls with God's word. All the more reason to carefully test the water of the wells we frequent. Where we find little to no Scripture, we are bound to find little to no blessing.

The best well of all is the Bible itself. We would do well to dive daily, prayerfully into its waters and drink as deeply as we are able. Doing so ensures that our flawed thinking will be renewed, releasing us to bear every bit of the fruit God intends.

_____

_____

_____

_____

_____

_____

_____

_____

_____

_____

_____

Psalm 2

¹Why do the nations rage and the peoples plot in vain?
²The kings of the earth set themselves, and the rulers take counsel together, against the Lord and against his Anointed, saying,
³"Let us burst their bonds apart and cast away their cords from us."
⁴He who sits in the heavens laughs; the Lord holds them in derision.
⁵Then he will speak to them in his wrath, and terrify them in his fury, saying,
⁶"As for me, I have set my King on Zion, my holy hill."
⁷I will tell of the decree: The Lord said to me, "You are my Son; today I have begotten you.
⁸Ask of me, and I will make the nations your heritage, and the ends of the earth your possession.
⁹You shall break them with a rod of iron and dash them in pieces like a potter's vessel."
¹⁰Now therefore, O kings, be wise; be warned, O rulers of the earth.
¹¹Serve the Lord with fear, and rejoice with trembling.
¹²Kiss the Son, lest he be angry, and you perish in the way, for his wrath is quickly kindled. Blessed are all who take refuge in him.

Housesitters

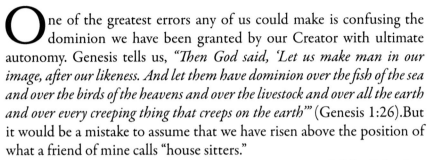

One of the greatest errors any of us could make is confusing the dominion we have been granted by our Creator with ultimate autonomy. Genesis tells us, *"Then God said, 'Let us make man in our image, after our likeness. And let them have dominion over the fish of the sea and over the birds of the heavens and over the livestock and over all the earth and over every creeping thing that creeps on the earth'"* (Genesis 1:26).But it would be a mistake to assume that we have risen above the position of what a friend of mine calls "house sitters."

In fact, that was at the heart of the temptation and fall of the first couple (Genesis 3). They bought into the lie that they could be like God and rival His loving authority over creation. Their failure didn't lead to life as they expected, but to the death God had promised.

The way of wisdom is to exercise every bit of the power God entrusts us as His stewards (employers, parents, coaches, civic leaders, team captains, board members, etc.) with the greatest of humility. Power of any kind is given us for the purpose of blessing not burdening those we influence; a privilege and responsibility. It is to be used ultimately for the purpose of exalting the One who allows us to have it in the first place.

"Blessed are all who take refuge in Him."

Psalm 3

A PSALM OF DAVID, WHEN HE FLED FROM ABSOLAM HIS SON.

¹O LORD, how many are my foes! Many are rising against me;
²many are saying of my soul, there is no salvation for him in
 God. Selah
³But you, O LORD, are a shield about me, my glory, and the lifter
 of my head.
⁴I cried aloud to the LORD, and he answered me from his holy
 hill. Selah
⁵I lay down and slept; I woke again, for the LORD sustained me.
⁶I will not be afraid of many thousands of people who have set
 themselves against me all around.
⁷Arise, O LORD! Save me, O my God! For you strike all my enemies on the cheek; you break the teeth of the wicked.
⁸Salvation belongs to the LORD; your blessing be on your
 people! Selah

Get Some Sleep

P anic.

"Sudden overpowering fright *also* : acute extreme anxiety; a sudden unreasoning terror." (Websters) Eyes wide ... heart racing ... gasping for air ... provoked by an imminent threat.

What next?

Is God the first or last place we run when life presses in? Is He our first call, or our last resort when all other options have failed? It is impossible to surprise Him. He is absolutely unrivaled by anyone or anything. He is a shield like no other for those who seek His protection. Yet still, bad things happen to the best of us. What are we to do?

Get some sleep.

What more beautiful expression of genuine dependence than to close our eyes in the greatest of vulnerability, entrusting ourselves to God, who delights to deliver us through life and death. Waking up can do wonders for our faith! Reminds me of a great story about a sleeping Savior on a boat in a great storm (Matthew 8:23-27).

"Why are you afraid, O you of little faith?"

_____
_____
_____
_____
_____
_____
_____
_____
_____
_____
_____

Psalm 4

To the choirmaster: with stringed instruments. A Psalm of David.

[1]Answer me when I call, O God of my righteousness! You have given me relief when I was in distress. Be gracious to me and hear my prayer!

[2]O men, how long shall my honor be turned into shame? How long will you love vain words and seek after lies? Selah

[3]But know that the Lord has set apart the godly for himself; the Lord hears when I call to him.

[4]Be angry, and do not sin; ponder in your own hearts on your beds, and be silent. Selah

[5]Offer right sacrifices, and put your trust in the Lord.

[6]There are many who say, "Who will show us some good? Lift up the light of your face upon us, O Lord!"

[7]You have put more joy in my heart than they have when their grain and wine abound.

[8]In peace I will both lie down and sleep; for you alone, O Lord, make me dwell in safety.

Devotion

If I'm honest, I want to be a higher priority in God's eyes than He is in mine. Forget the fact that He made me, not the other way around. I want to be of first importance on His list of "to do's", especially when life isn't going according to plan ... my plan.

I feel lots of liberty (to do as I please) when it comes to complying with God's revealed will, but would really like for Him to follow my wishes to the last letter.

Isn't it ironic? That I would demand devotion from my Creator which far surpasses the devotion I give to Him, especially in light of the devotion He has already shown me in the loving sacrifice of His Son.

When I'm in my right mind, I can't help but say with the Psalmist, "You have put more joy in my heart than [the many] have when their grain and wine abound." Oh that I would stay in my right mind more often every day.

_____

_____

_____

_____

_____

_____

_____

_____

_____

_____

Psalm 5

To the choirmaster: for the flutes. A Psalm of David.

¹Give ear to my words, O LORD; consider my groaning.

²Give attention to the sound of my cry, my King and my God, for to you do I pray.

³O LORD, in the morning you hear my voice; in the morning I prepare a sacrifice for you and watch.

⁴For you are not a God who delights in wickedness; evil may not dwell with you.

⁵The boastful shall not stand before your eyes; you hate all evildoers.

⁶You destroy those who speak lies; the LORD abhors the bloodthirsty and deceitful man.

⁷But I, through the abundance of your steadfast love, will enter your house. I will bow down toward your holy temple in the fear of you.

⁸Lead me, O LORD, in your righteousness because of my enemies; make your way straight before me.

⁹For there is no truth in their mouth; their inmost self is destruction; their throat is an open grave; they flatter with their tongue.

¹⁰Make them bear their guilt, O God; let them fall by their own counsels; because of the abundance of their transgressions cast them out, for they have rebelled against you.

¹¹But let all who take refuge in you rejoice; let them ever sing for joy, and spread your protection over them, that those who love your name may exult in you.

¹²For you bless the righteous, O LORD; you cover him with favor as with a shield.

Waging War

Enemies ... can't live with'em, can't live without'em. They come right along with life in a sin-wrecked world.

We cannot, must not live in fear of those who seek to undermine the good works God has given us to do. Nor should we gloss over antagonism as if it is meaningless. Enemies require confrontation.

How we go about doing that is of great importance.

Insult for insult erodes the strength of our standing. Slander and deception create a two-front battle, one with our enemy and another with our God. So if you can't join'em, beat'em (in a non-physical way of course).

"If God is for us, who can be against us?" (Romans 8:31) What better way to confront opposition than in the throne room of God! It may seem passive, but consider this: enlisting the infinite wisdom, power, protection and favor of a Holy God undaunted by the pitiful attempts of human rebellion.

Perhaps our greatest offense is eager reliance upon the Almighty's defense. #UNDEFEATED

_____
_____
_____
_____
_____
_____
_____
_____
_____
_____

Psalm 6

To the choirmaster: with stringed instruments; according to The Sheminith. A Psalm of David.

¹O Lord, rebuke me not in your anger, nor discipline me in your wrath.

²Be gracious to me, O Lord, for I am languishing; heal me, O Lord, for my bones are troubled.

³My soul also is greatly troubled. But you, O Lord—how long?

⁴Turn, O Lord, deliver my life; save me for the sake of your steadfast love.

⁵For in death there is no remembrance of you; in Sheol who will give you praise?

⁶I am weary with my moaning; every night I flood my bed with tears; I drench my couch with my weeping.

⁷My eye wastes away because of grief; it grows weak because of all my foes.

⁸Depart from me, all you workers of evil, for the Lord has heard the sound of my weeping.

⁹The Lord has heard my plea; the Lord accepts my prayer.

¹⁰All my enemies shall be ashamed and greatly troubled; they shall turn back and be put to shame in a moment.

The Gift Of Discipline

The discipline of God is among the most precious of gifts. Without it our stubborn, self-reliant hearts would settle for cheap worldly thrills when true, Spirit-sculpted joy could be had.

It is stunning how hard and painful life must get before most of us finally yield, surrender. God disciplines those He loves, and He loves us enough to bring us to the end of our miserable attempts at self-made lives (the greatest of delusions).

Ironically, when we hit bottom ("sick and tired of being sick and tired"), we ask, "How long O Lord?" As if He were late for a mandatory meeting.

I envision a gentle, knowing smile sweeping over the face of God. "I'm so glad you decided to join us."

_____
_____
_____
_____
_____
_____
_____
_____
_____
_____

Psalm 7

A Shiggaion of David, which he sang to the Lord concerning the words of Cush, a Benjaminite.

¹O Lord my God, in you do I take refuge; save me from all my pursuers and deliver me,
²lest like a lion they tear my soul apart, rending it in pieces, with none to deliver.
³O Lord my God, if I have done this, if there is wrong in my hands,
⁴if I have repaid my friend with evil or plundered my enemy without cause,
⁵let the enemy pursue my soul and overtake it, and let him trample my life to the ground and lay my glory in the dust. Selah
⁶Arise, O Lord, in your anger; lift yourself up against the fury of my enemies; awake for me; you have appointed a judgment.
⁷Let the assembly of the peoples be gathered about you; over it return on high.
⁸The Lord judges the peoples; judge me, O Lord, according to my righteousness and according to the integrity that is in me.
⁹Oh, let the evil of the wicked come to an end, and may you establish the righteous— you who test the minds and hearts, O righteous God!
¹⁰My shield is with God, who saves the upright in heart.
¹¹God is a righteous judge, and a God who feels indignation every day.
¹²If a man does not repent, God will whet his sword; he has bent and readied his bow;
¹³he has prepared for him his deadly weapons, making his arrows fiery shafts.
¹⁴Behold, the wicked man conceives evil and is pregnant with mischief and gives birth to lies.
¹⁵He makes a pit, digging it out, and falls into the hole that he has made.
¹⁶His mischief returns upon his own head, and on his own skull his violence descends.
¹⁷I will give to the Lord the thanks due to his righteousness, and I will sing praise to the name of the Lord, the Most High.

Justice For All

It's an easy thing to pray for the downfall of our opposition, whether in an athletic contest, a political debate, or in a case of personal injustice.

It's a hard thing to pray just as fervently for the justice of God in our own lives, against our own flaws and failures, whether we are aware of them or not.

While asking God for mercy, grace and favor to be shown to us, while asking God to render justice on our behalf, we would do well to invite His righteous light to shine on our hearts and reveal that which would require our own repentance. In this we preserve our own posture of humility and ensure that we pray soberly in alignment with the heart of God.

God is adamantly opposed to all that is unrighteous in our world and in our lives. It is in His holy nature to do so. May we be a people who pray eagerly that He would address both.

_____
_____
_____
_____
_____
_____
_____
_____
_____
_____
_____

Psalm 8

To the choirmaster: according to The Gittith.
A Psalm of David.

¹O Lord, our Lord, how majestic is your name in all the earth! You have set your glory above the heavens.
²Out of the mouth of babies and infants, you have established strength because of your foes, to still the enemy and the avenger.
³When I look at your heavens, the work of your fingers, the moon and the stars, which you have set in place,
⁴what is man that you are mindful of him, and the son of man that you care for him?
⁵Yet you have made him a little lower than the heavenly beings and crowned him with glory and honor.
⁶You have given him dominion over the works of your hands; you have put all things under his feet,
⁷all sheep and oxen, and also the beasts of the field,
⁸the birds of the heavens, and the fish of the sea, whatever passes along the paths of the seas.
⁹O Lord, our Lord, how majestic is your name in all the earth!

Search For Significance

I've heard that one of our greatest needs in life is to matter; to know that we are somehow significant. I get that, feel that, see that on a regular basis.

That craving, if not fed with truth leads to a couple of bad endings ... self-importance (an exaggeration) or self-contempt (an underestimation). Both conclusions are rooted in an attempt to find our significance in our own achievements. We assume we matter if we can point to something about us the world seems to value, and we assume we don't if we can't.

How strange that we would set our sights below the wonder of being made in the image of God. What could be more significant than being fashioned by the heart of God? Loved, animated, empowered, esteemed before having ever accomplished anything. Absolutely stunning really!

Our value isn't at all based upon the majesty we conjure, but upon the majesty of our Maker. It's amazing and assuring that One so grand would give us a second thought!

_____
_____
_____
_____
_____
_____
_____
_____
_____
_____

Psalm 9

TO THE CHOIRMASTER: ACCORDING TO MUTH-LABBEN.
A PSALM OF DAVID.

[1]I will give thanks to the LORD with my whole heart; I will recount all of your wonderful deeds.
[2]I will be glad and exult in you; I will sing praise to your name, O Most High.
[3]When my enemies turn back, they stumble and perish before your presence.
[4]For you have maintained my just cause; you have sat on the throne, giving righteous judgment.
[5]You have rebuked the nations; you have made the wicked perish; you have blotted out their name forever and ever.
[6]The enemy came to an end in everlasting ruins; their cities you rooted out; the very memory of them has perished.
[7]But the LORD sits enthroned forever; he has established his throne for justice,
[8]and he judges the world with righteousness; he judges the peoples with uprightness.
[9]The LORD is a stronghold for the oppressed, a stronghold in times of trouble.
[10]And those who know your name put their trust in you, for you, O LORD, have not forsaken those who seek you.
[11]Sing praises to the LORD, who sits enthroned in Zion! Tell among the peoples his deeds!
[12]For he who avenges blood is mindful of them; he does not forget the cry of the afflicted.
[13]Be gracious to me, O LORD! See my affliction from those who hate me, O you who lift me up from the gates of death,
[14]that I may recount all your praises, that in the gates of the daughter of Zion I may rejoice in your salvation.
[15]The nations have sunk in the pit that they made; in the net that they hid, their own foot has been caught.
[16]The LORD has made himself known; he has executed judgment; the wicked are snared in the work of their own hands. Higgaion. Selah
[17]The wicked shall return to Sheol, all the nations that forget God.
[18]For the needy shall not always be forgotten, and the hope of the poor shall not perish forever.
[19]Arise, O LORD! Let not man prevail; let the nations be judged before you!
[20]Put them in fear, O LORD! Let the nations know that they are but men! Selah

King Of Kings And Paupers

Thrones ... we just don't get'm in the good'ol USofA.

The great experiment of democracy (which I like by the way) doesn't at all help us grasp the nature of living under the rule of a king. Yet, the most common biblical reference to the spiritual realm in which we live is that of a kingdom with a King.

God's throne is eternal (admittedly hard to wrap our minds around). It has always existed and will have no end. God didn't ascend to His throne or topple a lesser god of some kind. He is and always has been absolutely sovereign, all-powerful, without rival.

He can run the universe any way He likes, and it turns out, He likes to protect the oppressed, comfort the afflicted, and sustain those who are needy. To those who use what power they have for their own purposes, He is a great adversary. To those who leverage their power for the good of others, He is a great friend.

It would do us all a lot of good to get better acquainted with the King of kings and the ways of His kingdom.

_____

_____

_____

_____

_____

_____

_____

_____

_____

_____

_____

Psalm 10

¹Why, O LORD, do you stand far away? Why do you hide yourself in times of trouble?

²In arrogance the wicked hotly pursue the poor; let them be caught in the schemes that they have devised.

³For the wicked boasts of the desires of his soul, and the one greedy for gain curses and renounces the LORD.

⁴In the pride of his face the wicked does not seek him; all his thoughts are, "There is no God."

⁵His ways prosper at all times; your judgments are on high, out of his sight; as for all his foes, he puffs at them.

⁶He says in his heart, "I shall not be moved; throughout all generations I shall not meet adversity."

⁷His mouth is filled with cursing and deceit and oppression; under his tongue are mischief and iniquity.

⁸He sits in ambush in the villages; in hiding places he murders the innocent. His eyes stealthily watch for the helpless;

⁹he lurks in ambush like a lion in his thicket; he lurks that he may seize the poor; he seizes the poor when he draws him into his net.

¹⁰The helpless are crushed, sink down, and fall by his might.

¹¹He says in his heart, "God has forgotten, he has hidden his face, he will never see it."

¹²Arise, O LORD; O God, lift up your hand; forget not the afflicted.

¹³Why does the wicked renounce God and say in his heart, "You will not call to account"?

¹⁴But you do see, for you note mischief and vexation, that you may take it into your hands; to you the helpless commits himself; you have been the helper of the fatherless.

¹⁵Break the arm of the wicked and evildoer; call his wickedness to account till you find none.

¹⁶The LORD is king forever and ever; the nations perish from his land.

¹⁷O LORD, you hear the desire of the afflicted; you will strengthen their heart; you will incline your ear

¹⁸to do justice to the fatherless and the oppressed, so that man who is of the earth may strike terror no more.

Invisible God

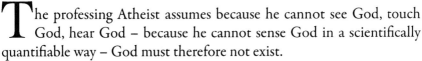

The professing Atheist assumes because he cannot see God, touch God, hear God – because he cannot sense God in a scientifically quantifiable way – God must therefore not exist.

Professing Christians often pray as if God cannot see, touch or hear what is taking place in His creation because they cannot scientifically verify His physical presence. And if He did see the pain, the suffering, the abuse that we see, wouldn't He step in!

What are we to do with an invisible God?

Overwhelming evidence that our universe (us included) has been intelligently designed exists all around us. Overwhelming evidence from history verifies that God has intruded over and again with redemptive purpose. And yet He goes often unseen.

Did He not answer the accusations of atheists and the plea of believers when he "took on flesh and dwelt among us" (John 1:14) ... when "blood and water" (John 19:34) spewed from His side after a brutal, humiliating, sin-covering death ... when He appeared to "more than 500" (1 Corinthians 15:6) after His resurrection.

Though we struggle to see Him, God doesn't struggle in the least to see us, to hear us, to know of our pain and bear it. Though He waits at the moment, He will one day break into our world with the greatest of presence and make all things new.

_____
_____
_____
_____
_____
_____
_____
_____
_____
_____
_____

Psalm 11

To the choirmaster. Of David.

[1]In the Lord I take refuge; how can you say to my soul, "Flee like a bird to your mountain,
[2]for behold, the wicked bend the bow; they have fitted their arrow to the string to shoot in the dark at the upright in heart;
[3]if the foundations are destroyed, what can the righteous do?"
[4]The Lord is in his holy temple; the Lord's throne is in heaven; his eyes see, his eyelids test the children of man.
[5]The Lord tests the righteous, but his soul hates the wicked and the one who loves violence.
[6]Let him rain coals on the wicked; fire and sulfur and a scorching wind shall be the portion of their cup.
[7]For the Lord is righteous; he loves righteous deeds; the upright shall behold his face.

Where Will You Run?

Life sure throws a lot at us.

The situations of a single day relentlessly press us, puzzle us, poke us, pull us, and propel us in the most surprising ways.

Options and opportunities appear like windows and doors, opening and closing, promising gain or threatening loss. Fight or flight? Hide or seek? Which way is the "right" way to run?

Perhaps God is less concerned about our being at the right place at the right time, and more concerned about our being the right man or woman for such a time and place as this ... wherever we might find ourselves.

We were not created merely to survive our circumstances, but to pass the tests of poverty and prosperity with hearts hungry for God. With Him as our refuge, our circumstances become a showcase ... not of our competence, but of the character God is forming in us.

_____

_____

_____

_____

_____

_____

_____

_____

_____

_____

Psalm 12

To the choirmaster: according to The Sheminith.
A Psalm of David.

[1]Save, O Lord, for the godly one is gone; for the faithful have vanished from among the children of man.
[2]Everyone utters lies to his neighbor; with flattering lips and a double heart they speak.
[3]May the Lord cut off all flattering lips, the tongue that makes great boasts,
[4]those who say, "With our tongue we will prevail, our lips are with us; who is master over us?"
[5]"Because the poor are plundered, because the needy groan, I will now arise," says the Lord; "I will place him in the safety for which he longs."
[6]The words of the Lord are pure words, like silver refined in a furnace on the ground, purified seven times.
[7]You, O Lord, will keep them; you will guard us from this generation forever.
[8]On every side the wicked prowl, as vileness is exalted among the children of man.

Cultural Minority

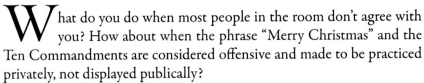

What do you do when most people in the room don't agree with you? How about when the phrase "Merry Christmas" and the Ten Commandments are considered offensive and made to be practiced privately, not displayed publically?

What do you do when the voice of the faithful have fallen to a whisper? When the voices heralding "alternative lifestyles" as the new normal boom in every direction? When sensuality is a cultural obsession, porn is a billion dollar a year industry, and sex trafficking is among the greatest social concerns.

What do you do when a culture is best described as "spiritual, but not religious?" When truth is reduced to personal preference? When the most fervent promoters of tolerance are decidedly intolerant toward any who don't think like them?

"Pray without ceasing" (1 Thessalonians 5:17).

Ask the Lord to preserve His people, however few they may be. Ask Him to fill the hearts of His followers with a resolve to stand firm on the truth of His word. Ask God to give His people endurance while swimming against the current of cultural relativism.

And after praying, don't be surprised when you are preserved ... emboldened ... strengthened. *"He will guard us from this generation forever."*

_____

_____

_____

_____

_____

_____

_____

_____

_____

_____

_____

Psalm 13

To the choirmaster. A Psalm of David.

[1]How long, O Lord? Will you forget me forever? How long will you hide your face from me?
[2]How long must I take counsel in my soul and have sorrow in my heart all the day? How long shall my enemy be exalted over me?
[3]Consider and answer me, O Lord my God; light up my eyes, lest I sleep the sleep of death,
[4]lest my enemy say, "I have prevailed over him," lest my foes rejoice because I am shaken.
[5]But I have trusted in your steadfast love; my heart shall rejoice in your salvation.
[6]I will sing to the Lord, because he has dealt bountifully with me.

Hide-n-Seek

Some days it feels like God has left the building.

Those are the days when things aren't going the way I'd like. I can handle a few of them at a time, but long stretches of suffering feel more like hide-n-seek with God than an episode of Father knows best. "Surely, if God were here with me, life wouldn't be this hard!"

The truth is, my earthly circumstances are poor proof of God's presence or absence. He has said, *"I will never leave you nor forsake you"* (Hebrews 13:5) ... good days or bad. If God seems distant or absent, it must be me, blinded by the sad reality of living in a sin-wrecked world.

Rather than looking for God as if He were missing, I'm always better off looking for the gift of growth He promises with His presence (Romans 8:28-29). Those gifts are often hard to see and even slower to arrive. But when they do, I find myself thinking, "It's just what I needed."

God truly has dealt bountifully with me.

_____
_____
_____
_____
_____
_____
_____
_____
_____
_____
_____

Psalm 14

¹The fool says in his heart, "There is no God." They are corrupt, they do abominable deeds, there is none who does good.
²The Lord looks down from heaven on the children of man, to see if there are any who understand, who seek after God.
³They have all turned aside; together they have become corrupt; there is none who does good, not even one.
⁴Have they no knowledge, all the evildoers who eat up my people as they eat bread and do not call upon the Lord?
⁵There they are in great terror, for God is with the generation of the righteous.
⁶You would shame the plans of the poor, but the Lord is his refuge.
⁷Oh, that salvation for Israel would come out of Zion! When the Lord restores the fortunes of his people, let Jacob rejoice, let Israel be glad.

Personal Hyperinflation

Few things are more damaging to the soul than empty optimism about the human condition. The power of positive thinking does nothing to correct our spiritual deficiency any more than a rabbit's foot can reverse the ravages of a terminal disease.

The only hope we have of genuine spiritual life isn't an inflated view of ourselves, but rather an honest admission of our hopelessness. The dead don't need stronger self-esteem, they need resurrection. There is One who can awaken us, raise us, restore us ... One who was and is and always will be all that we are not ... Almighty God.

_____

_____

_____

_____

_____

_____

_____

_____

_____

_____

Psalm 15

A PSALM OF DAVID.

[1]O LORD, who shall sojourn in your tent? Who shall dwell on your holy hill?
[2]He who walks blamelessly and does what is right and speaks truth in his heart;
[3]who does not slander with his tongue and does no evil to his neighbor, nor takes up a reproach against his friend;
[4]in whose eyes a vile person is despised, but who honors those who fear the LORD; who swears to his own hurt and does not change;
[5]who does not put out his money at interest and does not take a bribe against the innocent. He who does these things shall never be moved.

Blessing & Boundaries

Do I crave the blessing of God with only mild interest in the boundaries of God?

Do I plead for God's presence in my life, but ask Him to check His holiness at the door?

Do I minimize the gap between my profession of faith and my practice of faith?

Do I long for stability in my own life while carelessly (or even intentionally) causing disruption in the lives of those around me?

It stands to reason that only those who genuinely embrace the holy heart of God would find themselves held securely in the holy hands of God. Both, of course, are undeniable displays of the grace of God.

Psalm 16

A Miktam of David.

[1]Preserve me, O God, for in you I take refuge.
[2]I say to the LORD, "You are my Lord; I have no good apart from you."
[3]As for the saints in the land, they are the excellent ones, in whom is all my delight.
[4]The sorrows of those who run after another god shall multiply; their drink offerings of blood I will not pour out or take their names on my lips.
[5]The LORD is my chosen portion and my cup; you hold my lot.
[6]The lines have fallen for me in pleasant places; indeed, I have a beautiful inheritance.
[7]I bless the LORD who gives me counsel; in the night also my heart instructs me.
[8]I have set the LORD always before me; because he is at my right hand, I shall not be shaken.
[9]Therefore my heart is glad, and my whole being rejoices; my flesh also dwells secure.
[10]For you will not abandon my soul to Sheol, or let your holy one see corruption.
[11]You make known to me the path of life; in your presence there is fullness of joy; at your right hand are pleasures forevermore.

Glad Heart

Our world is infatuated with options, upgrades, and innovations ... all of which come with a promise to make our lives more efficient, effective, and enjoyable ... heaven on earth. I may have missed something, but despite several thousand years of "progress", evil, pain, suffering, injustice and death are as common today as they've ever been.

Creature comforts are nice, but they don't begin to approach the incomparable goodness God grants with His presence.

I have lost much, hurt deeply, feared greatly, sinned regrettably ... but I wouldn't exchange my story for another. I can't help but be awestruck by God's kindness toward one so undeserving as me. I can trace a long line of grace couriers sent by the Lord to comfort, correct, and counsel my frail and foolish soul.

Left to myself, I'd be lost. But a path to life has been shown me ... a path saturated with God's joyful presence ... a path I never have to walk alone. My heart is glad.

_____

_____

_____

_____

_____

_____

_____

_____

_____

_____

_____

Psalm 17
A Prayer of David.

[1]Hear a just cause, O Lord; attend to my cry! Give ear to my prayer from lips free of deceit!

[2]From your presence let my vindication come! Let your eyes behold the right!

[3]You have tried my heart, you have visited me by night, you have tested me, and you will find nothing; I have purposed that my mouth will not transgress.

[4]With regard to the works of man, by the word of your lips I have avoided the ways of the violent.

[5]My steps have held fast to your paths; my feet have not slipped.

[6]I call upon you, for you will answer me, O God; incline your ear to me; hear my words.

[7]Wondrously show your steadfast love, O Savior of those who seek refuge from their adversaries at your right hand.

[8]Keep me as the apple of your eye; hide me in the shadow of your wings,

[9]from the wicked who do me violence, my deadly enemies who surround me.

[10]They close their hearts to pity; with their mouths they speak arrogantly.

[11]They have now surrounded our steps; they set their eyes to cast us to the ground.

[12]He is like a lion eager to tear, as a young lion lurking in ambush.

[13]Arise, O Lord! Confront him, subdue him! Deliver my soul from the wicked by your sword,

[14]from men by your hand, O Lord, from men of the world whose portion is in this life. You fill their womb with treasure; they are satisfied with children, and they leave their abundance to their infants.

[15]As for me, I shall behold your face in righteousness; when I awake, I shall be satisfied with your likeness.

Loose Lips

Careless words can be devastating.

In WWII, great efforts were made to warn of how costly careless conversation could be. Strategic secrets in enemy hands often led to lost lives. **"Loose Lips Might Sink Ships"** became a national call to restraint.

Reminds me of a phrase I first heard from Dennis Rainey years ago ... ***"Loose lips Sink Relationships."*** I can't hope to experience intimacy with God and others if I am unwilling to yield control of my tongue to the guidance of God's Spirit. On the other hand, I sure have a lot more confidence seeking blessing when my requests are accompanied by words I've already spoken, prompted by God for the good of others.

The apostle Peter put his foot in his mouth as much as any of the disciples, yet near the end of his life he wrote, *"Whoever desires to love life and see good days, let him keep his tongue from evil and his lips from speaking deceit."* (1 Peter 3:10) I know of no greater guardrail than the goal of building up rather than tearing down with what I say. *"Let no corrupting talk come out of your mouths, but only such as is good for building up, as fits the occasion, that it may give grace to those who hear."* (Ephesians 4:29)

_____

_____

_____

_____

_____

_____

_____

_____

_____

_____

_____

Psalm 18

To the choirmaster. A Psalm of David, the servant of the Lord, who addressed the words of this song to the Lord on the day when the Lord rescued him from the hand of all his enemies, and from the hand of Saul. He said:

¹I love you, O LORD, my strength.

²The LORD is my rock and my fortress and my deliverer, my God, my rock, in whom I take refuge, my shield, and the horn of my salvation, my stronghold.

³I call upon the LORD, who is worthy to be praised, and I am saved from my enemies.

⁴The cords of death encompassed me; the torrents of destruction assailed me;

⁵the cords of Sheol entangled me; the snares of death confronted me.

⁶In my distress I called upon the LORD; to my God I cried for help. From his temple he heard my voice, and my cry to him reached his ears.

⁷Then the earth reeled and rocked; the foundations also of the mountains trembled and quaked, because he was angry.

⁸Smoke went up from his nostrils, and devouring fire from his mouth; glowing coals flamed forth from him.

⁹He bowed the heavens and came down; thick darkness was under his feet.

¹⁰He rode on a cherub and flew; he came swiftly on the wings of the wind.

¹¹He made darkness his covering, his canopy around him, thick clouds dark with water.

¹²Out of the brightness before him hailstones and coals of fire broke through his clouds.

¹³The LORD also thundered in the heavens, and the Most High uttered his voice, hailstones and coals of fire.

¹⁴And he sent out his arrows and scattered them; he flashed forth lightnings and routed them.

¹⁵Then the channels of the sea were seen, and the foundations of the world were laid bare at your rebuke, O LORD, at the blast of the breath of your nostrils.

[16]He sent from on high, he took me; he drew me out of many waters.

[17]He rescued me from my strong enemy and from those who hated me, for they were too mighty for me.

[18]They confronted me in the day of my calamity, but the LORD was my support.

[19]He brought me out into a broad place; he rescued me, because he delighted in me.

[20]The LORD dealt with me according to my righteousness; according to the cleanness of my hands he rewarded me.

[21]For I have kept the ways of the LORD, and have not wickedly departed from my God.

[22]For all his rules were before me, and his statutes I did not put away from me.

[23]I was blameless before him, and I kept myself from my guilt.

[24]So the LORD has rewarded me according to my righteousness, according to the cleanness of my hands in his sight.

[25]With the merciful you show yourself merciful; with the blameless man you show yourself blameless;

[26]with the purified you show yourself pure; and with the crooked you make yourself seem tortuous.

[27]For you save a humble people, but the haughty eyes you bring down.

[28]For it is you who light my lamp; the LORD my God lightens my darkness.

[29]For by you I can run against a troop, and by my God I can leap over a wall.

[30]This God—his way is perfect; the word of the LORD proves true; he is a shield for all those who take refuge in him.

[31]For who is God, but the LORD? And who is a rock, except our God?—

[32]the God who equipped me with strength and made my way blameless.

[33]He made my feet like the feet of a deer and set me secure on the heights.

[34]He trains my hands for war, so that my arms can bend a bow of bronze.

[35]You have given me the shield of your salvation, and your right hand supported me, and your gentleness made me great.

[36]You gave a wide place for my steps under me, and my feet did not slip.

[37]I pursued my enemies and overtook them, and did not turn back till they were consumed.

[38]I thrust them through, so that they were not able to rise; they fell under my feet.

[39]For you equipped me with strength for the battle; you made those who rise against me sink under me.

[40]You made my enemies turn their backs to me, and those who hated me I destroyed.

[41]They cried for help, but there was none to save; they cried to the LORD, but he did not answer them.

[42]I beat them fine as dust before the wind; I cast them out like the mire of the streets.

[43]You delivered me from strife with the people; you made me the head of the nations; people whom I had not known served me.

[44]As soon as they heard of me they obeyed me; foreigners came cringing to me.

[45]Foreigners lost heart and came trembling out of their fortresses.

[46]The LORD lives, and blessed be my rock, and exalted be the God of my salvation—

[47]the God who gave me vengeance and subdued peoples under me,

[48]who delivered me from my enemies; yes, you exalted me above those who rose against me; you rescued me from the man of violence.

[49]For this I will praise you, O LORD, among the nations, and sing to your name.

[50]Great salvation he brings to his king, and shows steadfast love to his anointed, to David and his offspring forever.

If God Is For Us

What would have to be true of God in order for me to trust Him? Omniscient (All-Knowing); Omnipotent (All Powerful); Omnipresent (Simultaneously Everywhere Present); Holy, loving, sovereign, merciful, wise ...

There's a long list of attributes that make God trustworthy. However, if I'm not a beneficiary of those attributes, I would trust Him as much as I would trust a god who is nothing more than a figment of someone else's imagination.

All in all, God must be real, He must be supreme, but if He is not for me, I could never truly trust Him. I don't mean that in the sense that He is "on my team." I mean that He intends to exercise His attributes for my good.

He is *for* all who are *with* Him ... trusting, following by grace, full of faith. We are *with* Him because He is *for* us. I love how the apostle Paul puts it:

"If God is for us, who can be against us? ... Who shall separate us from the love of Christ? Shall tribulation, or distress, or persecution, or famine, or nakedness, or danger, or sword? ... For I am sure that neither death nor life, nor angels nor rulers, nor things present nor things to come, nor powers, nor height nor depth, nor anything else in all creation, will be able to separate us from the love of God in Christ Jesus our Lord." (Romans 8:31-39)

"The LORD is my rock and my fortress and my deliverer, my God, my rock, in whom I take refuge, my shield, and the horn of my salvation, my stronghold." (Psalm 18:2)

_____
_____
_____
_____
_____
_____
_____

Psalm 19

To the choirmaster. A Psalm of David.

¹The heavens declare the glory of God, and the sky above proclaims his handiwork.

²Day to day pours out speech, and night to night reveals knowledge.

³There is no speech, nor are there words, whose voice is not heard.

⁴Their voice goes out through all the earth, and their words to the end of the world. In them he has set a tent for the sun,

⁵which comes out like a bridegroom leaving his chamber, and, like a strong man, runs its course with joy.

⁶Its rising is from the end of the heavens, and its circuit to the end of them, and there is nothing hidden from its heat.

⁷The law of the LORD is perfect, reviving the soul; the testimony of the LORD is sure, making wise the simple;

⁸the precepts of the LORD are right, rejoicing the heart; the commandment of the LORD is pure, enlightening the eyes;

⁹the fear of the LORD is clean, enduring forever; the rules of the LORD are true, and righteous altogether.

¹⁰More to be desired are they than gold, even much fine gold; sweeter also than honey and drippings of the honeycomb.

¹¹Moreover, by them is your servant warned; in keeping them there is great reward.

¹²Who can discern his errors? Declare me innocent from hidden faults.

¹³Keep back your servant also from presumptuous sins; let them not have dominion over me! Then I shall be blameless, and innocent of great transgression.

¹⁴Let the words of my mouth and the meditation of my heart be acceptable in your sight, O LORD, my rock and my redeemer.

A Word From Our Creator

Truth is discovered not determined by humanity. We don't make the sun rise and fall. Turns out, our speck of a planet rotates while following its precise, invisible track through our speck of a solar system, within our speck of a galaxy, dwarfed by a universe we've hardly begun to comprehend.

Our world literally and figuratively revolves around the sun. Without it we go dark, we freeze, we die. With it we have light, vision, life.

We lack light and life without a word from our Creator as much as we would without the sun He created. But our darkness is self-inflicted. We strive to independently feel our way through the darkness while a great beacon is within our grasp.

God's word doesn't limit my potential. It doesn't cramp my style. It doesn't quash my creativity ... Quite the opposite! The Scriptures revive, renew, refine, and restore a heart wandering in the dark. The Bible contains far more than witty words or philosophical ideals. It is food for my soul, revealing to me afresh each day the Son around whom my life revolves with every breath I take.

_____

_____

_____

_____

_____

_____

_____

_____

_____

_____

_____

Psalm 20

To the choirmaster. A Psalm of David.

[1]May the Lord answer you in the day of trouble! May the name of the God of Jacob protect you!
[2]May he send you help from the sanctuary and give you support from Zion!
[3]May he remember all your offerings and regard with favor your burnt sacrifices! Selah
[4]May he grant you your heart's desire and fulfill all your plans!
[5]May we shout for joy over your salvation, and in the name of our God set up our banners! May the Lord fulfill all your petitions!
[6]Now I know that the Lord saves his anointed; he will answer him from his holy heaven with the saving might of his right hand.
[7]Some trust in chariots and some in horses, but we trust in the name of the Lord our God.
[8]They collapse and fall, but we rise and stand upright.
[9]O Lord, save the king! May he answer us when we call.

Asking And Receiving

God is free to act in any way He wants that is consistent with His nature and character.

I am free (by God's design) to act upon the opportunities life gives me, some good, some not.

I am always free to ask for Gods favor, God's blessing, God's provision and protection. But I cannot expect God to move on my behalf simply because I ask. I may be asking for something that is inconsistent with His nature and character.

Before I ask, I should pause to consider whether or not my request is in alignment with God's heart, His good and perfect will for me and this world in which I live. When I ask, I should always be glad to receive a reply of "wait" or "no." **As His child, God always has my best interests in mind, even when I don't understand.**

I can be most confident when I am most interested in seeing His will accomplished than I am my own. I am "saved" amid my circumstances when I am trusting entirely in Him and not in myself or the resources I possess.

This I know, *"The eyes of the LORD run to and fro throughout the whole earth, to give strong support to those whose heart is blameless toward him"* (2 Chronicles 16:9). **Our God will always give us what we need to do what He has called us to do.**

_____
_____
_____
_____
_____
_____
_____
_____
_____
_____
_____

Psalm 21

To the choirmaster. A Psalm of David.

¹O LORD, in your strength the king rejoices, and in your salvation how greatly he exults!

²You have given him his heart's desire and have not withheld the request of his lips. Selah

³For you meet him with rich blessings; you set a crown of fine gold upon his head.

⁴He asked life of you; you gave it to him, length of days forever and ever.

⁵His glory is great through your salvation; splendor and majesty you bestow on him.

⁶For you make him most blessed forever; you make him glad with the joy of your presence.

⁷For the king trusts in the LORD, and through the steadfast love of the Most High he shall not be moved.

⁸Your hand will find out all your enemies; your right hand will find out those who hate you.

⁹You will make them as a blazing oven when you appear. The LORD will swallow them up in his wrath, and fire will consume them.

¹⁰You will destroy their descendants from the earth, and their offspring from among the children of man.

¹¹Though they plan evil against you, though they devise mischief, they will not succeed.

¹²For you will put them to flight; you will aim at their faces with your bows.

¹³Be exalted, O LORD, in your strength! We will sing and praise your power.

Unmoved Mover

Strength is currency in the world of assurance.

Absolute strength (and the assurance it affords) in any context is about being immovable and moving all else at will. We naturally feel safe and secure to the degree that we believe we cannot be threatened by a force greater than our own.

In reality, we are truly fragile creatures, who cling to whatever strength we possess, knowing it can be overcome by any number of opposing forces. We are not indestructible, incorruptible, or unyielding. We are mortal.

Genuine assurance is not found in us, but in the ultimate Unmoved Mover. His strength goes far beyond merely securing the present; rather it stretches on into eternity.

_____

_____

_____

_____

_____

_____

_____

_____

_____

_____

_____

Psalm 22

To the choirmaster: according to The Doe of the Dawn.
A Psalm of David.

¹My God, my God, why have you forsaken me? Why are you so far from saving me, from the words of my groaning?

²O my God, I cry by day, but you do not answer, and by night, but I find no rest.

³Yet you are holy, enthroned on the praises of Israel.

⁴In you our fathers trusted; they trusted, and you delivered them.

⁵To you they cried and were rescued; in you they trusted and were not put to shame.

⁶But I am a worm and not a man, scorned by mankind and despised by the people.

⁷All who see me mock me; they make mouths at me; they wag their heads;

⁸"He trusts in the LORD; let him deliver him; let him rescue him, for he delights in him!"

⁹Yet you are he who took me from the womb; you made me trust you at my mother's breasts.

¹⁰On you was I cast from my birth, and from my mother's womb you have been my God.

¹¹Be not far from me, for trouble is near, and there is none to help.

¹²Many bulls encompass me; strong bulls of Bashan surround me;

¹³they open wide their mouths at me, like a ravening and roaring lion.

¹⁴I am poured out like water, and all my bones are out of joint; my heart is like wax; it is melted within my breast;

¹⁵my strength is dried up like a potsherd, and my tongue sticks to my jaws; you lay me in the dust of death.

¹⁶For dogs encompass me; a company of evildoers encircles me; they have pierced my hands and feet—

¹⁷I can count all my bones— they stare and gloat over me;

¹⁸they divide my garments among them, and for my clothing they cast lots.

¹⁹But you, O LORD, do not be far off! O you my help, come quickly to my aid!

²⁰Deliver my soul from the sword, my precious life from the power of the dog!

²¹Save me from the mouth of the lion! You have rescued me from the horns of the wild oxen!

²²I will tell of your name to my brothers; in the midst of the congregation I will praise you:

²³You who fear the LORD, praise him! All you offspring of Jacob, glorify him, and stand in awe of him, all you offspring of Israel!

²⁴For he has not despised or abhorred the affliction of the afflicted, and he has not hidden his face from him, but has heard, when he cried to him.

²⁵From you comes my praise in the great congregation; my vows I will perform before those who fear him.

²⁶The afflicted shall eat and be satisfied; those who seek him shall praise the LORD! May your hearts live forever!

²⁷All the ends of the earth shall remember and turn to the LORD, and all the families of the nations shall worship before you.

²⁸For kingship belongs to the LORD, and he rules over the nations.

²⁹All the prosperous of the earth eat and worship; before him shall bow all who go down to the dust, even the one who could not keep himself alive.

³⁰Posterity shall serve him; it shall be told of the Lord to the coming generation;

³¹they shall come and proclaim his righteousness to a people yet unborn, that he has done it.

Our Savior's Song

"Eli eli lama sabachthani" ... My God, my God, why have you forsaken me?"

After 33 years of enduring life sinlessly in a broken, sin-wrecked world; betrayal by one of His own; a charade of a trial conducted by His chosen people; mockery, humiliation, and merciless abuse; hanging bloody on a cross pierced by nails, suffering perhaps the most gruesome execution devised by man ... Jesus quotes the words of Psalm 22 declaring the true cost of his sacrificial death ... becoming the object of God the Father's wrath poured out against sin and death.

2 Corinthians 5:21 *For our sake he made him to be sin who knew no sin, so that in him we might become the righteousness of God.*

"How deep the Father's love for us; how vast beyond all measure. That He should give His only Son to make a wretch His treasure." – lyrics by Stuart Townend

I marvel at the Father, Son and Spirit devising so sweet a gift to save my soul even while I was their enemy, a sinner fixed upon having life on my terms. Oh that my life would be a steady song of gratitude for that which I could never repay, but only receive by grace through faith.

_____

_____

_____

_____

Psalm 23

A Psalm of David.

¹The Lord is my shepherd; I shall not want.

²He makes me lie down in green pastures. He leads me beside still waters.

³He restores my soul. He leads me in paths of righteousness for his name's sake.

⁴Even though I walk through the valley of the shadow of death, I will fear no evil, for you are with me; your rod and your staff, they comfort me.

⁵You prepare a table before me in the presence of my enemies; you anoint my head with oil; my cup overflows.

⁶Surely goodness and mercy shall follow me all the days of my life, and I shall dwell in the house of the Lord forever.

A Sheep's Diary

Sheep without a shepherd are doomed.

Sheep with an incompetent shepherd are vulnerable at best.

Sheep with a good shepherd, despite all their natural flaws and frailties, are assured nourishment, renewal, security and fruitfulness they could not have otherwise.

I do not suffer for lack of a good shepherd; I suffer from my lack of awareness of my desperate need for Him. Thankfully, His goodness and mercy are so vast, He moves heaven and earth to retrieve me from wandering.

The Lord is my Shepherd ... and I shall dwell in the house of the Lord forever.

_____

_____

_____

_____

_____

_____

_____

_____

_____

_____

Psalm 24

A PSALM OF DAVID.

[1]The earth is the LORD's and the fullness thereof, the world and those who dwell therein,
[2]for he has founded it upon the seas and established it upon the rivers.
[3]Who shall ascend the hill of the LORD? And who shall stand in his holy place?
[4]He who has clean hands and a pure heart, who does not lift up his soul to what is false and does not swear deceitfully.
[5]He will receive blessing from the LORD and righteousness from the God of his salvation.
[6]Such is the generation of those who seek him, who seek the face of the God of Jacob. Selah
[7]Lift up your heads, O gates! And be lifted up, O ancient doors, that the King of glory may come in.
[8]Who is this King of glory? The LORD, strong and mighty, the LORD, mighty in battle!
[9]Lift up your heads, O gates! And lift them up, O ancient doors, that the King of glory may come in.
[10]Who is this King of glory? The LORD of hosts, he is the King of glory! Selah

Meet Your Maker

We frown upon people full of themselves; people puffed up with a warped sense of their greatness.

It's strange for the finite to act infinite, especially when the Infinite One is everywhere present; kind of embarrassing really.

We make far better stewards than owners. Running the universe is out of our league, but managing a small corner of the world for the One who made it all (and made us all); it's what we were made for.

Blessing comes to those who seek their Maker instead of striving to be self-made. Our significance is found in celebrating the breath-taking beauty of the One whose likeness we bear ... the Lord of hosts. He is the King of glory.

_____

_____

_____

_____

_____

_____

_____

_____

_____

Psalm 25

Of David.

¹To you, O Lord, I lift up my soul.

²O my God, in you I trust; let me not be put to shame; let not my enemies exult over me.

³Indeed, none who wait for you shall be put to shame; they shall be ashamed who are wantonly treacherous.

⁴Make me to know your ways, O Lord; teach me your paths.

⁵Lead me in your truth and teach me, for you are the God of my salvation; for you I wait all the day long.

⁶Remember your mercy, O Lord, and your steadfast love, for they have been from of old.

⁷Remember not the sins of my youth or my transgressions; according to your steadfast love remember me, for the sake of your goodness, O Lord!

⁸Good and upright is the Lord; therefore he instructs sinners in the way.

⁹He leads the humble in what is right, and teaches the humble his way.

¹⁰All the paths of the Lord are steadfast love and faithfulness, for those who keep his covenant and his testimonies.

¹¹For your name's sake, O Lord, pardon my guilt, for it is great.

¹²Who is the man who fears the Lord? Him will he instruct in the way that he should choose.

¹³His soul shall abide in well-being, and his offspring shall inherit the land.

¹⁴The friendship of the Lord is for those who fear him, and he makes known to them his covenant.

¹⁵My eyes are ever toward the Lord, for he will pluck my feet out of the net.

¹⁶Turn to me and be gracious to me, for I am lonely and afflicted.

¹⁷The troubles of my heart are enlarged; bring me out of my distresses.

¹⁸Consider my affliction and my trouble, and forgive all my sins.

¹⁹Consider how many are my foes, and with what violent hatred they hate me.

²⁰Oh, guard my soul, and deliver me! Let me not be put to shame, for I take refuge in you.

²¹May integrity and uprightness preserve me, for I wait for you.

²²Redeem Israel, O God, out of all his troubles.

Help!

Just ask God for help.

The reasons are many that I don't ... I think I can handle it; I should be able to handle it; I want to handle it myself; I doubt if asking for help will do any good; I don't deserve help after the mess I've made; I'm going to look/feel really stupid if God doesn't do what I want Him to do.

I guess at the end of the day, trusting in myself seems like a better wager than trusting in God. But my story says otherwise. I've let myself down countless times, but I can't think of a time when I've regretted putting things into God's hands. I am my own worst enemy, and God is my greatest friend.

"None who wait for God (trust in; look to; hope in; expectantly rely on; faithfully follow) *will be put to shame."* Is it too good to be true? Not a chance.

I will never have a need so small or great that God will not gladly take it on and meet my dependence with His unfailing sufficiency, full of mercy and grace.

_____

_____

_____

_____

_____

_____

_____

_____

_____

Psalm 26
OF DAVID.

[1]Vindicate me, O LORD, for I have walked in my integrity, and I have trusted in the LORD without wavering.

[2]Prove me, O LORD, and try me; test my heart and my mind.

[3]For your steadfast love is before my eyes, and I walk in your faithfulness.

[4]I do not sit with men of falsehood, nor do I consort with hypocrites.

[5]I hate the assembly of evildoers, and I will not sit with the wicked.

[6]I wash my hands in innocence and go around your altar, O LORD,

[7]proclaiming thanksgiving aloud, and telling all your wondrous deeds.

[8]O LORD, I love the habitation of your house and the place where your glory dwells.

[9]Do not sweep my soul away with sinners, nor my life with bloodthirsty men,

[10]in whose hands are evil devices, and whose right hands are full of bribes.

[11]But as for me, I shall walk in my integrity; redeem me, and be gracious to me.

[12]My foot stands on level ground; in the great assembly I will bless the LORD.

Hold Fast

I am unquestionably at my best when I cling tightly to my Savior. Clinging isn't just a state of mind. It is active, visceral, responsive and concrete.

It looks like integrity, trust, perseverance, submission, and gratitude. It's intentional movement toward the righteous will of God. It means that my daily activities, ordinary and unusual are infused with a heart of shameless adoration for the One who animates my every act of obedience with His grace.

Even at my best, especially at my best, I need to humbly invite the Lord to "test my heart and my mind" so that I might not be blindsided by the residue of rebellion that lurks in my flesh.

Spiritual confidence and consistency is only had by those who keep their gaze fixed on the steadfast, sustaining love of Christ. Assurance is found in nothing else.

_____
_____
_____
_____
_____
_____
_____
_____
_____

Psalm 27
Of David.

[1]The LORD is my light and my salvation; whom shall I fear? The LORD is the stronghold of my life; of whom shall I be afraid?

[2]When evildoers assail me to eat up my flesh, my adversaries and foes, it is they who stumble and fall.

[3]Though an army encamp against me, my heart shall not fear; though war arise against me, yet I will be confident.

[4]One thing have I asked of the LORD, that will I seek after: that I may dwell in the house of the LORD all the days of my life, to gaze upon the beauty of the LORD and to inquire in his temple.

[5]For he will hide me in his shelter in the day of trouble; he will conceal me under the cover of his tent; he will lift me high upon a rock.

[6]And now my head shall be lifted up above my enemies all around me, and I will offer in his tent sacrifices with shouts of joy; I will sing and make melody to the LORD.

[7]Hear, O LORD, when I cry aloud; be gracious to me and answer me!

[8]You have said, "Seek my face." My heart says to you, "Your face, LORD, do I seek."

[9]Hide not your face from me. Turn not your servant away in anger, O you who have been my help. Cast me not off; forsake me not, O God of my salvation!

[10]For my father and my mother have forsaken me, but the LORD will take me in.

[11]Teach me your way, O LORD, and lead me on a level path because of my enemies.

[12]Give me not up to the will of my adversaries; for false witnesses have risen against me, and they breathe out violence.

[13]I believe that I shall look upon the goodness of the LORD in the land of the living!

[14]Wait for the LORD; be strong, and let your heart take courage; wait for the LORD!

Wartime

An undeniable battle is raging all around us. Dress it up, bleach it, spray it down with a little cologne; It's still ugly, soiled, and smells of hostility and death. The stakes aren't land, castles, power or prosperity ... they're much higher.

I awake every single day, not to a spiritual truce or "cease fire." I come under the relentless attack of an unseen enemy utterly devoted to my destruction. *"We do not wrestle against flesh and blood, but against the rulers, against the authorities, against the cosmic powers over this present darkness, against the spiritual forces of evil in the heavenly places."* (Ephesians 6:12)

I possess no hope of survival apart from the God of my salvation. He alone is my hiding place. He alone equips me for a battle I cannot avoid or ignore. He bids me, *"Put on the whole armor of God, that you may be able to stand against the schemes of the devil."* (Ephesians 6:10)

Complacency is concession, surrender ... loss. Today, by God's grace and in the strength of His might, I will fight the good fight knowing that a day is coming when *"I shall look upon the goodness of the Lord in the land of the living!"* (Psalm 27:13)

_____
_____
_____
_____
_____
_____
_____
_____
_____
_____

Psalm 28

OF DAVID.

[1]To you, O LORD, I call; my rock, be not deaf to me, lest, if you be silent to me, I become like those who go down to the pit.
[2]Hear the voice of my pleas for mercy, when I cry to you for help, when I lift up my hands toward your most holy sanctuary.
[3]Do not drag me off with the wicked, with the workers of evil, who speak peace with their neighbors while evil is in their hearts.
[4]Give to them according to their work and according to the evil of their deeds; give to them according to the work of their hands; render them their due reward.
[5]Because they do not regard the works of the LORD or the work of his hands, he will tear them down and build them up no more.
[6]Blessed be the LORD! For he has heard the voice of my pleas for mercy.
[7]The LORD is my strength and my shield; in him my heart trusts, and I am helped; my heart exults, and with my song I give thanks to him.
[8]The LORD is the strength of his people; he is the saving refuge of his anointed.
[9]Oh, save your people and bless your heritage! Be their shepherd and carry them forever.

What If?

What if God did not listen?
What if God did not care?
What if God were not merciful?

We would be without grace, forgiveness, restoration, power and hope. We would have no Savior. We would be left with nothing more than the best this life has to offer and nothing less than condemnation when this life is done.

But God does listen. He does care. He is full of mercy. He is the Good Shepherd.

Call to Him. Cry for help. Lift your hands toward His most holy Sanctuary.

"Cast all your anxieties on Him because He cares for you." (1 Peter 5:7)

_____
_____
_____
_____
_____
_____
_____
_____
_____
_____

Psalm 29

A Psalm of David.

¹Ascribe to the LORD, O heavenly beings, ascribe to the LORD glory and strength.
²Ascribe to the LORD the glory due his name; worship the LORD in the splendor of holiness.
³The voice of the LORD is over the waters; the God of glory thunders, the LORD, over many waters.
⁴The voice of the LORD is powerful; the voice of the LORD is full of majesty.
⁵The voice of the LORD breaks the cedars; the LORD breaks the cedars of Lebanon.
⁶He makes Lebanon to skip like a calf, and Sirion like a young wild ox.
⁷The voice of the LORD flashes forth flames of fire.
⁸The voice of the LORD shakes the wilderness; the LORD shakes the wilderness of Kadesh.
⁹The voice of the LORD makes the deer give birth and strips the forests bare, and in his temple all cry, "Glory!"
¹⁰The LORD sits enthroned over the flood; the LORD sits enthroned as king forever.
¹¹May the LORD give strength to his people! May the LORD bless his people with peace!

A Gift For The Giver

What do you give the One who has everything? Not just any one, THE ONE. *The Creator of all things, in heaven and on earth, visible and invisible, whether thrones or dominions or rulers or authorities ... the One in whom all things hold together.* (Colossians 1:16-17) That One!

He is absolutely self-sufficient, absent of even the slightest existence of need. Talk about tough to buy for! Could He possibly want anything I might give Him?

How about giving Him the gift that suits Him perfectly ... Glory. It comes in all shapes, sizes, colors and styles; magnifying His beauty in the most beautiful way.

Honor, praise, and adoration all fit Him like a glove! And worship is on His "wish-list" not because He is in any way deficient without it, but because all things (including us) find and fulfill their highest aim when exalting the only One worthy of such accolades.

_____

_____

_____

_____

_____

_____

_____

_____

_____

_____

Psalm 30

A Psalm of David. A song at the dedication of the temple.

¹I will extol you, O Lord, for you have drawn me up and have not let my foes rejoice over me.
²O Lord my God, I cried to you for help, and you have healed me.
³O Lord, you have brought up my soul from Sheol; you restored me to life from among those who go down to the pit.
⁴Sing praises to the Lord, O you his saints, and give thanks to his holy name.
⁵For his anger is but for a moment, and his favor is for a lifetime. Weeping may tarry for the night, but joy comes with the morning.
⁶As for me, I said in my prosperity, "I shall never be moved."
⁷By your favor, O Lord, you made my mountain stand strong; you hid your face; I was dismayed.
⁸To you, O Lord, I cry, and to the Lord I plead for mercy:
⁹"What profit is there in my death, if I go down to the pit? Will the dust praise you? Will it tell of your faithfulness?
¹⁰Hear, O Lord, and be merciful to me! O Lord, be my helper!"
¹¹You have turned for me my mourning into dancing; you have loosed my sackcloth and clothed me with gladness,
¹²that my glory may sing your praise and not be silent. O Lord my God, I will give thanks to you forever!

Hard Lessons

How easy it is to fail the test of prosperity.

Success can be so intoxicating. It whispers in my heart, "Invincible! ... Untouchable! ... King of the world!" I become enamored with my own thoughts and grow apathetic toward renewing my mind with truth that resides with God, not me. Such deception is devastating!

With the greatest of affection, God allows me to experience the pain of self-reliance. I'm shown the deficiency and danger of life on my own. *"The Lord disciplines the one He loves, and chastises every son whom He receives ... for our good."* (Hebrews 12:6, 10) Thankfully, His discipline ends when my dependence resumes.

Pain is a profound tutor, but not my eternal companion. It guides me back to the sufficiency of my Savior where I find the joy I believed was found apart from Him.

_____

_____

_____

_____

_____

_____

_____

_____

_____

_____

Psalm 31

To the choirmaster. A Psalm of David.

[1]In you, O LORD, do I take refuge; let me never be put to shame; in your righteousness deliver me!

[2]Incline your ear to me; rescue me speedily! Be a rock of refuge for me, a strong fortress to save me!

[3]For you are my rock and my fortress; and for your name's sake you lead me and guide me;

[4]you take me out of the net they have hidden for me, for you are my refuge.

[5]Into your hand I commit my spirit; you have redeemed me, O LORD, faithful God.

[6]I hate those who pay regard to worthless idols, but I trust in the LORD.

[7]I will rejoice and be glad in your steadfast love, because you have seen my affliction; you have known the distress of my soul,

[8]and you have not delivered me into the hand of the enemy; you have set my feet in a broad place.

[9]Be gracious to me, O LORD, for I am in distress; my eye is wasted from grief; my soul and my body also.

[10]For my life is spent with sorrow, and my years with sighing; my strength fails because of my iniquity, and my bones waste away.

[11]Because of all my adversaries I have become a reproach, especially to my neighbors, and an object of dread to my acquaintances; those who see me in the street flee from me.

[12]I have been forgotten like one who is dead; I have become like a broken vessel.

[13]For I hear the whispering of many— terror on every side!— as they scheme together against me, as they plot to take my life.

[14]But I trust in you, O LORD; I say, "You are my God."

[15]My times are in your hand; rescue me from the hand of my enemies and from my persecutors!

[16]Make your face shine on your servant; save me in your steadfast love!

[17]O LORD, let me not be put to shame, for I call upon you; let the wicked be put to shame; let them go silently to Sheol.

[18]Let the lying lips be mute, which speak insolently against the righteous in pride and contempt.

[19]Oh, how abundant is your goodness, which you have stored up for those who fear you and worked for those who take refuge in you, in the sight of the children of mankind!

[20]In the cover of your presence you hide them from the plots of men; you store them in your shelter from the strife of tongues.

²¹Blessed be the LORD, for he has wondrously shown his steadfast love to me when I was in a besieged city.

²²I had said in my alarm, "I am cut off from your sight." But you heard the voice of my pleas for mercy when I cried to you for help.

²³Love the LORD, all you his saints! The LORD preserves the faithful but abundantly repays the one who acts in pride.

²⁴Be strong, and let your heart take courage, all you who wait for the LORD!

Live Like You're Dying

It wasn't just the way He died.

Luke 23:46 *"Then Jesus, calling out with a loud voice, said, "Father, into your hands I commit my spirit!" And having said this he breathed his last."*

It was the way He lived every moment of His earthly life. Every act of kindness, every step of obedience, every word spoken, every miracle wrought; all done in absolute dependence upon the Father and Spirit He had known for all of eternity past. His greatest desire was to fulfill the desire of the One who sent Him.

John 6:38 *"I have come down from heaven, not to do my own will but the will of him who sent me."*

Surely my will is inferior to the will of my Maker. To think otherwise is absurd. I am most secure when I am most attentive to His guidance and most reliant upon His care ... not only on my deathbed, but along every twist and turn of my journey through life.

Psalm 31:19 *"Oh, how abundant is HIS goodness, which HE has stored up for those who fear HIM and worked for those who take refuge in HIM, in the sight of the children of mankind!"*

_____

_____

_____

_____

_____

_____

Psalm 32

A Maskil of David.

¹Blessed is the one whose transgression is forgiven, whose sin is covered.

²Blessed is the man against whom the LORD counts no iniquity, and in whose spirit there is no deceit.

³For when I kept silent, my bones wasted away through my groaning all day long.

⁴For day and night your hand was heavy upon me; my strength was dried up as by the heat of summer. Selah

⁵I acknowledged my sin to you, and I did not cover my iniquity; I said, "I will confess my transgressions to the LORD," and you forgave the iniquity of my sin. Selah

⁶Therefore let everyone who is godly offer prayer to you at a time when you may be found; surely in the rush of great waters, they shall not reach him.

⁷You are a hiding place for me; you preserve me from trouble; you surround me with shouts of deliverance. Selah

⁸I will instruct you and teach you in the way you should go; I will counsel you with my eye upon you.

⁹Be not like a horse or a mule, without understanding, which must be curbed with bit and bridle, or it will not stay near you.

¹⁰Many are the sorrows of the wicked, but steadfast love surrounds the one who trusts in the LORD.

¹¹Be glad in the LORD, and rejoice, O righteous, and shout for joy, all you upright in heart!

The Great Cover Up

I hide my sin two ways. One keeps it out of site but leaves it to spread like a cancer. The other way covers and quarantines my sin so that its deadly affect can be remedied.

The first is an elaborate strategy of deception, smoke and mirrors if you will. I draw attention to what is right and good so as to conceal what lingers in the dark. My offenses are swiftly justified, minimized, sanitized or denied, leaving transgressions and their ravaging effects untreated.

What an exhausting exercise in futility! Though hidden from plain site, sin never escapes the holy gaze of God. He can't help but shed light on it in hopes of repentance, a change of heart.

Rather than striving on my own to cover what cannot go unseen, why not ask God to cover what cannot go unaddressed? He invites me to bring what is hidden into plain view. *"Come now, let us reason together, says the LORD: though your sins are like scarlet, they shall be as white as snow."* (Isaiah 1:18)

Honest admission, confession transfers my transgressions to the only One who can conceal them. He does so with His own shed blood, the ransom for my rebellion. *"All we like sheep have gone astray; we have turned—every one—to his own way; and the LORD has laid on him the iniquity of us all."* (Isaiah 53:6)

"Therefore let everyone who is godly offer prayer to Him at a time when He may be found." (Psalm 32:6)

_____

_____

_____

_____

_____

_____

_____

_____

_____

Psalm 33

¹Shout for joy in the LORD, O you righteous! Praise befits the upright.

²Give thanks to the LORD with the lyre; make melody to him with the harp of ten strings!

³Sing to him a new song; play skillfully on the strings, with loud shouts.

⁴For the word of the LORD is upright, and all his work is done in faithfulness.

⁵He loves righteousness and justice; the earth is full of the steadfast love of the LORD.

⁶By the word of the LORD the heavens were made, and by the breath of his mouth all their host.

⁷He gathers the waters of the sea as a heap; he puts the deeps in storehouses.

⁸Let all the earth fear the LORD; let all the inhabitants of the world stand in awe of him!

⁹For he spoke, and it came to be; he commanded, and it stood firm.

¹⁰The LORD brings the counsel of the nations to nothing; he frustrates the plans of the peoples.

¹¹The counsel of the LORD stands forever, the plans of his heart to all generations.

¹²Blessed is the nation whose God is the LORD, the people whom he has chosen as his heritage!

¹³The LORD looks down from heaven; he sees all the children of man;

¹⁴from where he sits enthroned he looks out on all the inhabitants of the earth,

¹⁵he who fashions the hearts of them all and observes all their deeds.

¹⁶The king is not saved by his great army; a warrior is not delivered by his great strength.

¹⁷The war horse is a false hope for salvation, and by its great might it cannot rescue.

¹⁸Behold, the eye of the LORD is on those who fear him, on those who hope in his steadfast love,

¹⁹that he may deliver their soul from death and keep them alive in famine.

²⁰Our soul waits for the LORD; he is our help and our shield.

²¹For our heart is glad in him, because we trust in his holy name.

²²Let your steadfast love, O LORD, be upon us, even as we hope in you.

Where's The Love?

Nothing lasts. Color fades, landscapes erode, structures deteriorate, and health declines ... every living thing eventually dies. Maintenance and repair is a necessity to extend the life of just about anything, but no amount of care ensures permanence.

It is within and throughout this broken, fragile, defective world that the steadfast love of God can be found. In fact, the earth is full of it! And contrary to its surroundings, it is stable, enduring, robust and infinite. It requires no maintenance and repair. It doesn't erode in the least. It is instrumental in sustaining all of life.

I shudder to think of what this world would be like in its absence. There is no substitute, no alternative that could ever suffice.

It's no wonder the Apostle Paul prays in his letter to the Ephesians, *"That you, being rooted and grounded in love, may have strength to comprehend with all the saints what is the breadth and length and height and depth, and to know the love of Christ that surpasses knowledge, that you may be filled with all the fullness of God."* (Ephesians 3:17-19)

_____

_____

_____

_____

_____

_____

_____

_____

_____

_____

Psalm 34

OF DAVID, WHEN HE CHANGED HIS BEHAVIOR BEFORE ABIMELECH, SO THAT HE DROVE HIM OUT, AND HE WENT AWAY.

¹I will bless the LORD at all times; his praise shall continually be in my mouth.

²My soul makes its boast in the LORD; let the humble hear and be glad.

³Oh, magnify the LORD with me, and let us exalt his name together!

⁴I sought the LORD, and he answered me and delivered me from all my fears.

⁵Those who look to him are radiant, and their faces shall never be ashamed.

⁶This poor man cried, and the LORD heard him and saved him out of all his troubles.

⁷The angel of the LORD encamps around those who fear him, and delivers them.

⁸Oh, taste and see that the LORD is good! Blessed is the man who takes refuge in him!

⁹Oh, fear the LORD, you his saints, for those who fear him have no lack!

¹⁰The young lions suffer want and hunger; but those who seek the LORD lack no good thing.

¹¹Come, O children, listen to me; I will teach you the fear of the LORD.

¹²What man is there who desires life and loves many days, that he may see good?

¹³Keep your tongue from evil and your lips from speaking deceit.

¹⁴Turn away from evil and do good; seek peace and pursue it.

¹⁵The eyes of the LORD are toward the righteous and his ears toward their cry.

¹⁶The face of the LORD is against those who do evil, to cut off the memory of them from the earth.

¹⁷When the righteous cry for help, the LORD hears and delivers them out of all their troubles.

¹⁸The LORD is near to the brokenhearted and saves the crushed in spirit.

¹⁹Many are the afflictions of the righteous, but the LORD delivers him out of them all.

²⁰He keeps all his bones; not one of them is broken.

²¹Affliction will slay the wicked, and those who hate the righteous will be condemned.

²²The LORD redeems the life of his servants; none of those who take refuge in him will be condemned.

Taste And See

I know life is difficult.

I've given out under the weight of despair.

I've felt unspeakable humiliation and shame.

I've been so afraid I could hardly breathe; so enraged I couldn't see straight.

My past warrants nothing better than merciless condemnation.

I know life is difficult. And that is why I beg of you, I plead with all my heart, *"Taste and see that the Lord is good."* He alone can give you hope, esteem your life with dignity, calm your fear, soothe your rage, and form the broken pieces of your past into a breathtaking mosaic of beauty.

God's goodness is the grandest of feasts. You're invited to find your seat at the table and partake. Taste ... trust ... take hold of the life that can be found in no other.

_____
_____
_____
_____
_____
_____
_____
_____
_____

Psalm 35

OF DAVID.

[1]Contend, O LORD, with those who contend with me; fight against those who fight against me!

[2]Take hold of shield and buckler and rise for my help!

[3]Draw the spear and javelin against my pursuers! Say to my soul, "I am your salvation!"

[4]Let them be put to shame and dishonor who seek after my life! Let them be turned back and disappointed who devise evil against me!

[5]Let them be like chaff before the wind, with the angel of the LORD driving them away!

[6]Let their way be dark and slippery, with the angel of the LORD pursuing them!

[7]For without cause they hid their net for me; without cause they dug a pit for my life.

[8]Let destruction come upon him when he does not know it! And let the net that he hid ensnare him; let him fall into it—to his destruction!

[9]Then my soul will rejoice in the LORD, exulting in his salvation.

[10]All my bones shall say, "O LORD, who is like you, delivering the poor from him who is too strong for him, the poor and needy from him who robs him?"

[11]Malicious witnesses rise up; they ask me of things that I do not know.

[12]They repay me evil for good; my soul is bereft.

[13]But I, when they were sick— I wore sackcloth; I afflicted myself with fasting; I prayed with head bowed on my chest.

[14]I went about as though I grieved for my friend or my brother; as one who laments his mother, I bowed down in mourning.

[15]But at my stumbling they rejoiced and gathered; they gathered together against me; wretches whom I did not know tore at me without ceasing;

[16]like profane mockers at a feast, they gnash at me with their teeth.

[17]How long, O Lord, will you look on? Rescue me from their destruction, my precious life from the lions!

[18]I will thank you in the great congregation; in the mighty throng I will praise you.

[19]Let not those rejoice over me who are wrongfully my foes, and let not those wink the eye who hate me without cause.

[20]For they do not speak peace, but against those who are quiet in the land they devise words of deceit.

[21]They open wide their mouths against me; they say, "Aha, Aha! Our eyes have seen it!"

[22]You have seen, O LORD; be not silent! O Lord, be not far from me!

²³Awake and rouse yourself for my vindication, for my cause, my God and my Lord!

²⁴Vindicate me, O Lord, my God, according to your righteousness, and let them not rejoice over me!

²⁵Let them not say in their hearts, "Aha, our heart's desire!" Let them not say, "We have swallowed him up."

²⁶Let them be put to shame and disappointed altogether who rejoice at my calamity! Let them be clothed with shame and dishonor who magnify themselves against me!

²⁷Let those who delight in my righteousness shout for joy and be glad and say evermore, "Great is the Lord, who delights in the welfare of his servant!"

²⁸Then my tongue shall tell of your righteousness and of your praise all the day long.

The Great Contender

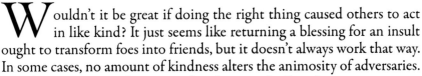

Wouldn't it be great if doing the right thing caused others to act in like kind? It just seems like returning a blessing for an insult ought to transform foes into friends, but it doesn't always work that way. In some cases, no amount of kindness alters the animosity of adversaries.

The temptation then is to abandon goodwill and resort to aggression; give'm a taste of their own medicine. That will teach them!

But in doing so, we sacrifice our character. We take matters into our own hands and sink to the level of our enemies. Better to stay our course, maintain our high ground and pray for vindication; easy to say and hard to do!

God is far more capable of preserving us and dealing with bullies. He actually delights in coming to the aid of those who would trust Him to be the guardian He promises to be.

_____

_____

_____

_____

_____

_____

Psalm 36

To the choirmaster. Of David, the servant of the Lord.

¹Transgression speaks to the wicked deep in his heart; there is no fear of God before his eyes.
²For he flatters himself in his own eyes that his iniquity cannot be found out and hated.
³The words of his mouth are trouble and deceit; he has ceased to act wisely and do good.
⁴He plots trouble while on his bed; he sets himself in a way that is not good; he does not reject evil.
⁵Your steadfast love, O Lord, extends to the heavens, your faithfulness to the clouds.
⁶Your righteousness is like the mountains of God; your judgments are like the great deep; man and beast you save, O Lord.
⁷How precious is your steadfast love, O God! The children of mankind take refuge in the shadow of your wings.
⁸They feast on the abundance of your house, and you give them drink from the river of your delights.
⁹For with you is the fountain of life; in your light do we see light.
¹⁰Oh, continue your steadfast love to those who know you, and your righteousness to the upright of heart!
¹¹Let not the foot of arrogance come upon me, nor the hand of the wicked drive me away.
¹²There the evildoers lie fallen; they are thrust down, unable to rise.

Two Paths

Evil is a dead end street. It gives the impression of freedom, power, assurance, cunning and control but leads to bondage, foolishness, misery and despair. To traffic in wickedness is to travel without light, careening through treacherous terrain into a grisly destination.

What little exhilaration one might feel evaporates when the wayward joyride comes to an abrupt stop.

There is another path paved with the steadfast love of God ... loyal and enduring. Those who follow it are infused with light, vision, and wisdom. They are able to see their way through the trials of a painfully wretched world. They find themselves traveling under the watchful care of the One who will surely deliver them into the infinite abundance of His presence.

Wise are those who think less about the ease or difficulty of their present location and more about the place the path they follow will take them.

_____
_____
_____
_____
_____
_____
_____
_____
_____
_____

Psalm 37

Of David.

¹Fret not yourself because of evildoers; be not envious of wrongdoers!

²For they will soon fade like the grass and wither like the green herb.

³Trust in the Lord, and do good; dwell in the land and befriend faithfulness.

⁴Delight yourself in the Lord, and he will give you the desires of your heart.

⁵Commit your way to the Lord; trust in him, and he will act.

⁶He will bring forth your righteousness as the light, and your justice as the noonday.

⁷Be still before the Lord and wait patiently for him; fret not yourself over the one who prospers in his way, over the man who carries out evil devices!

⁸Refrain from anger, and forsake wrath! Fret not yourself; it tends only to evil.

⁹For the evildoers shall be cut off, but those who wait for the Lord shall inherit the land.

¹⁰In just a little while, the wicked will be no more; though you look carefully at his place, he will not be there.

¹¹But the meek shall inherit the land and delight themselves in abundant peace.

¹²The wicked plots against the righteous and gnashes his teeth at him,

¹³but the Lord laughs at the wicked, for he sees that his day is coming.

¹⁴The wicked draw the sword and bend their bows to bring down the poor and needy, to slay those whose way is upright;

¹⁵their sword shall enter their own heart, and their bows shall be broken.

¹⁶Better is the little that the righteous has than the abundance of many wicked.

¹⁷For the arms of the wicked shall be broken, but the Lord upholds the righteous.

[18]The LORD knows the days of the blameless, and their heritage will remain forever;

[19]they are not put to shame in evil times; in the days of famine they have abundance.

[20]But the wicked will perish; the enemies of the LORD are like the glory of the pastures; they vanish—like smoke they vanish away.

[21]The wicked borrows but does not pay back, but the righteous is generous and gives;

[22]for those blessed by the LORD shall inherit the land, but those cursed by him shall be cut off.

[23]The steps of a man are established by the LORD, when he delights in his way;

[24]though he fall, he shall not be cast headlong, for the LORD upholds his hand.

[25]I have been young, and now am old, yet I have not seen the righteous forsaken or his children begging for bread.

[26]He is ever lending generously, and his children become a blessing.

[27]Turn away from evil and do good; so shall you dwell forever.

[28]For the LORD loves justice; he will not forsake his saints. They are preserved forever, but the children of the wicked shall be cut off.

[29]The righteous shall inherit the land and dwell upon it forever.

[30]The mouth of the righteous utters wisdom, and his tongue speaks justice.

[31]The law of his God is in his heart; his steps do not slip.

[32]The wicked watches for the righteous and seeks to put him to death.

[33]The LORD will not abandon him to his power or let him be condemned when he is brought to trial.

[34]Wait for the LORD and keep his way, and he will exalt you to inherit the land; you will look on when the wicked are cut off.

[35]I have seen a wicked, ruthless man, spreading himself like a green laurel tree.

[36]But he passed away, and behold, he was no more; though I sought him, he could not be found.

[37]Mark the blameless and behold the upright, for there is a future for the man of peace.

[38]But transgressors shall be altogether destroyed; the future of the wicked shall be cut off.

[39]The salvation of the righteous is from the LORD; he is their stronghold in the time of trouble.

[40]The LORD helps them and delivers them; he delivers them from the wicked and saves them, because they take refuge in him.

Heart's Desire

What do you want?

So many things in this life rival for the affections our heart. This world serves up an endless supply of shiny, new and improved trinkets that tickle our taste for immediate gratification. How easily we believe that acquisition and consumption of temporary devices will satisfy our insatiable appetite.

I want more, but more of what? Be careful what you wish for.

How about this ... who do you want? The Lord can give you anything and everything; He owns it all. But more than mere stuff, He longs to give you that which truly quenches the thirst of your soul. **He longs to give you Himself.**

Anything less will leave you wanting. Anything less will leave you wasting away in a pointless pursuit of lesser things. *"Delight yourself in the LORD, and he will give you the desires of your heart."* (Psalm 37:4)

Psalm 38

A PSALM OF DAVID, FOR THE MEMORIAL OFFERING.

[1]O LORD, rebuke me not in your anger, nor discipline me in your wrath!
[2]For your arrows have sunk into me, and your hand has come down on me.
[3]There is no soundness in my flesh because of your indignation; there is no health in my bones because of my sin.
[4]For my iniquities have gone over my head; like a heavy burden, they are too heavy for me.
[5]My wounds stink and fester because of my foolishness,
[6]I am utterly bowed down and prostrate; all the day I go about mourning.
[7]For my sides are filled with burning, and there is no soundness in my flesh.
[8]I am feeble and crushed; I groan because of the tumult of my heart.
[9]O Lord, all my longing is before you; my sighing is not hidden from you.
[10]My heart throbs; my strength fails me, and the light of my eyes—it also has gone from me.
[11]My friends and companions stand aloof from my plague, and my nearest kin stand far off.
[12]Those who seek my life lay their snares; those who seek my hurt speak of ruin and meditate treachery all day long.
[13]But I am like a deaf man; I do not hear, like a mute man who does not open his mouth.
[14]I have become like a man who does not hear, and in whose mouth are no rebukes.
[15]But for you, O LORD, do I wait; it is you, O Lord my God, who will answer.
[16]For I said, "Only let them not rejoice over me, who boast against me when my foot slips!"
[17]For I am ready to fall, and my pain is ever before me.
[18]I confess my iniquity; I am sorry for my sin.
[19]But my foes are vigorous, they are mighty, and many are those who hate me wrongfully.
[20]Those who render me evil for good accuse me because I follow after good.
[21]Do not forsake me, O LORD! O my God, be not far from me!
[22]Make haste to help me, O Lord, my salvation!

The Bottom

It's hard to tell when someone, even we ourselves hit bottom. There are usually several false bottoms preceding the giant thud when the last shoe drops.

Sin is ugly business. It leads us along like a pimp, using us while keeping us using; sustaining us with our idol of choice until we find ourselves face down in a sewer only God knows where ... the bottom.

Ironically, it is in that dark, lonely, hopeless place where life is often reborn. All is lost – pride, self-reliance, deceit, addiction – making room for the ultimate gain, genuine spiritual life.

From one sinner to another, the bottom is that glorious moment when we are finally (as the old saying goes) sick and tired of being sick and tired.

Are we there yet?

Psalm 39

To the choirmaster: to Jeduthun. A Psalm of David.

¹I said, "I will guard my ways, that I may not sin with my tongue; I will guard my mouth with a muzzle, so long as the wicked are in my presence."

²I was mute and silent; I held my peace to no avail, and my distress grew worse.

³My heart became hot within me. As I mused, the fire burned; then I spoke with my tongue:

⁴"O Lord, make me know my end and what is the measure of my days; let me know how fleeting I am!

⁵Behold, you have made my days a few handbreadths, and my lifetime is as nothing before you. Surely all mankind stands as a mere breath! Selah

⁶Surely a man goes about as a shadow! Surely for nothing they are in turmoil; man heaps up wealth and does not know who will gather!

⁷"And now, O Lord, for what do I wait? My hope is in you.

⁸Deliver me from all my transgressions. Do not make me the scorn of the fool!

⁹I am mute; I do not open my mouth, for it is you who have done it.

¹⁰Remove your stroke from me; I am spent by the hostility of your hand.

¹¹When you discipline a man with rebukes for sin, you consume like a moth what is dear to him; surely all mankind is a mere breath! Selah

¹²"Hear my prayer, O Lord, and give ear to my cry; hold not your peace at my tears! For I am a sojourner with you, a guest, like all my fathers.

¹³Look away from me, that I may smile again, before I depart and am no more!"

Make It Count

The average life expectancy is the U.S. right now is 78 years. Seems like forever to a teenager, a knock on the door to a senior adult. Subtract the time we spend sleeping, we've got about five decades to do whatever it is we're going to do with our short stint on earth.

Strange isn't it, how reckless we are with our days when we have what seems to be an endless supply.

I suppose one of the best ways to make the most of our days is to be mindful of how few of them we truly have and how significant each of them truly are. Hours become priceless when they are meager and an eternity awaits. Days are wasted when they are treated with contempt, taken for granted, consumed without thought of their eternal value.

By God's abundant grace, may we make every thought, word and deed rich in righteousness for now and forevermore.

_____

_____

_____

_____

_____

_____

_____

_____

_____

Psalm 40

To the choirmaster. A Psalm of David.

¹I waited patiently for the Lord; he inclined to me and heard my cry.
²He drew me up from the pit of destruction, out of the miry bog, and set my feet upon a rock, making my steps secure.
³He put a new song in my mouth, a song of praise to our God. Many will see and fear, and put their trust in the Lord.
⁴Blessed is the man who makes the Lord his trust, who does not turn to the proud, to those who go astray after a lie!
⁵You have multiplied, O Lord my God, your wondrous deeds and your thoughts toward us; none can compare with you! I will proclaim and tell of them, yet they are more than can be told.
⁶In sacrifice and offering you have not delighted, but you have given me an open ear. Burnt offering and sin offering you have not required.
⁷Then I said, "Behold, I have come; in the scroll of the book it is written of me:
⁸I delight to do your will, O my God; your law is within my heart."
⁹I have told the glad news of deliverance in the great congregation; behold, I have not restrained my lips, as you know, O Lord.
¹⁰I have not hidden your deliverance within my heart; I have spoken of your faithfulness and your salvation; I have not concealed your steadfast love and your faithfulness from the great congregation.
¹¹As for you, O Lord, you will not restrain your mercy from me; your steadfast love and your faithfulness will ever preserve me!
¹²For evils have encompassed me beyond number; my iniquities have overtaken me, and I cannot see; they are more than the hairs of my head; my heart fails me.
¹³Be pleased, O Lord, to deliver me! O Lord, make haste to help me!
¹⁴Let those be put to shame and disappointed altogether who seek to snatch away my life; let those be turned back and brought to dishonor who delight in my hurt!
¹⁵Let those be appalled because of their shame who say to me, "Aha, Aha!"
¹⁶But may all who seek you rejoice and be glad in you; may those who love your salvation say continually, "Great is the Lord!"
¹⁷As for me, I am poor and needy, but the Lord takes thought for me. You are my help and my deliverer; do not delay, O my God!

Symphony Of Salvation

There is nothing sweeter than the song of the redeemed.

The score of a great symphony is composed when one is lifted from the depths of destruction and mercifully set upon a sure foundation.

Notes of praise ring out from the lips of those delivered, honoring the Savior who showered love on them when it was not the least bit deserved. The joyful song effortlessly echoes in the halls of humanity, a declaration of adoration from the unashamed.

The world strives to muffle the melody of those who have been saved, but the great Conductor plays on through the lives of those who trust in Him to rescue again and again.

_____

_____

_____

_____

_____

_____

_____

_____

_____

_____

Psalm 41

To the choirmaster. A Psalm of David.

¹Blessed is the one who considers the poor! In the day of trouble the Lord delivers him;
²the Lord protects him and keeps him alive; he is called blessed in the land; you do not give him up to the will of his enemies.
³The Lord sustains him on his sickbed; in his illness you restore him to full health.
⁴As for me, I said, "O Lord, be gracious to me; heal me, for I have sinned against you!"
⁵My enemies say of me in malice, "When will he die, and his name perish?"
⁶And when one comes to see me, he utters empty words, while his heart gathers iniquity; when he goes out, he tells it abroad.
⁷All who hate me whisper together about me; they imagine the worst for me.
⁸They say, "A deadly thing is poured out on him; he will not rise again from where he lies."
⁹Even my close friend in whom I trusted, who ate my bread, has lifted his heel against me.
¹⁰But you, O Lord, be gracious to me, and raise me up, that I may repay them!
¹¹By this I know that you delight in me: my enemy will not shout in triumph over me.
¹²But you have upheld me because of my integrity, and set me in your presence forever.
¹³Blessed be the Lord, the God of Israel, from everlasting to everlasting! Amen and Amen.

Spiritual Life Support

I learned at a very young age to be a survivor. I sought to assert myself as strong, assured, and invincible against all manner of attack. Humanity marvels at the self-made.

Later I learned that I'm on spiritual life support and I have an adversary (along with every other man, woman and child) who knows my vulnerabilities. He finds great satisfaction in exploiting my frailty. He takes pleasure in accusing me of my inability to advance without aid.

While helpless in and of myself, I am not without hope.

I am sustained by the strength of Another, the Lord who made me in His image. He alone is able to heal my broken heart. He alone can restore my feeble will to walk well. He alone is able to steady my hands for the good fight.

It is only because of Him, *the author and perfecter of my faith* (Hebrews 12:2), I will survive the onslaught of my enemy.

_____
_____
_____
_____
_____
_____
_____
_____
_____
_____

Psalm 42

To the choirmaster. A Maskil of the Sons of Korah.

[1]As a deer pants for flowing streams, so pants my soul for you, O God.
[2]My soul thirsts for God, for the living God. When shall I come and appear before God?
[3]My tears have been my food day and night, while they say to me all the day long, "Where is your God?"
[4]These things I remember, as I pour out my soul: how I would go with the throng and lead them in procession to the house of God with glad shouts and songs of praise, a multitude keeping festival.
[5]Why are you cast down, O my soul, and why are you in turmoil within me? Hope in God; for I shall again praise him, my salvation
[6]and my God. My soul is cast down within me; therefore I remember you from the land of Jordan and of Hermon, from Mount Mizar.
[7]Deep calls to deep at the roar of your waterfalls; all your breakers and your waves have gone over me.
[8]By day the LORD commands his steadfast love, and at night his song is with me, a prayer to the God of my life.
[9]I say to God, my rock: "Why have you forgotten me? Why do I go mourning because of the oppression of the enemy?"
[10]As with a deadly wound in my bones, my adversaries taunt me, while they say to me all the day long, "Where is your God?"
[11]Why are you cast down, O my soul, and why are you in turmoil within me? Hope in God; for I shall again praise him, my salvation and my God.

Homesick

It's tough being in a faraway place, estranged from all that we hold dear. Familiar people and practices saturated with faith, hope and love infuse us with strength, contentment, purpose and joy. Without them our hearts can easily grow lonely, weary and depressed, languishing in despair.

Even worse is being surrounded in exile by voices of mockery and contempt. "Where is your God now?"

What better relief for a homesick heart than the truth that our way through the wilderness will eventually lead us home again in this life or the next. Our joyous past is but a taste of our glorious future in community with God and His people.

_____
_____
_____
_____
_____
_____
_____
_____
_____
_____

Psalm 43

[1]Vindicate me, O God, and defend my cause against an ungodly people, from the deceitful and unjust man deliver me!
[2]For you are the God in whom I take refuge; why have you rejected me? Why do I go about mourning because of the oppression of the enemy?
[3]Send out your light and your truth; let them lead me; let them bring me to your holy hill and to your dwelling!
[4]Then I will go to the altar of God, to God my exceeding joy, and I will praise you with the lyre, O God, my God.
[5]Why are you cast down, O my soul, and why are you in turmoil within me? Hope in God; for I shall again praise him, my salvation and my God.

A Way Of Escape

Temptation is so alluring when life gets tough ... a moment of relief, a sugary substitute, a way of escape. Pain certainly heightens our awareness, even our appreciation for all things pleasurable. And if iniquity weren't somehow pleasurable, well then, it wouldn't be the least bit attractive.

But compromise comes with a cost. Sin offers deliverance and then shackles the suckers who take the bait.

In the fog of fear and frustration, we are wise to look for light not leisure. We do well to set our gaze far and wide beyond our circumstances in search of a "straight path" (Proverbs 3:5-6). The God-honoring way through hardship is always available, just hard to see through distorted desires.

No temptation has overtaken you that is not common to man. God is faithful, and he will not let you be tempted beyond your ability, but with the temptation he will also provide the way of escape, that you may be able to endure it. (1 Corinthians 10:13)

_____
_____
_____
_____
_____
_____
_____
_____
_____
_____

Psalm 44

To the choirmaster. A Maskil of the Sons of Korah.

¹O God, we have heard with our ears, our fathers have told us, what deeds you performed in their days, in the days of old:

²you with your own hand drove out the nations, but them you planted; you afflicted the peoples, but them you set free;

³for not by their own sword did they win the land, nor did their own arm save them, but your right hand and your arm, and the light of your face, for you delighted in them.

⁴You are my King, O God; ordain salvation for Jacob!

⁵Through you we push down our foes; through your name we tread down those who rise up against us.

⁶For not in my bow do I trust, nor can my sword save me.

⁷But you have saved us from our foes and have put to shame those who hate us.

⁸In God we have boasted continually, and we will give thanks to your name forever. Selah

⁹But you have rejected us and disgraced us and have not gone out with our armies.

¹⁰You have made us turn back from the foe, and those who hate us have gotten spoil.

¹¹You have made us like sheep for slaughter and have scattered us among the nations.

¹²You have sold your people for a trifle, demanding no high price for them.

¹³You have made us the taunt of our neighbors, the derision and scorn of those around us.

¹⁴You have made us a byword among the nations, a laughingstock among the peoples.

¹⁵All day long my disgrace is before me, and shame has covered my face

¹⁶at the sound of the taunter and reviler, at the sight of the enemy and the avenger.

¹⁷All this has come upon us, though we have not forgotten you, and we have not been false to your covenant.

¹⁸Our heart has not turned back, nor have our steps departed from your way;

¹⁹yet you have broken us in the place of jackals and covered us with the shadow of death.

²⁰If we had forgotten the name of our God or spread out our hands to a foreign god,

²¹would not God discover this? For he knows the secrets of the heart.

²²Yet for your sake we are killed all the day long; we are regarded as sheep to be slaughtered.

²³Awake! Why are you sleeping, O Lord? Rouse yourself! Do not reject us forever!

²⁴Why do you hide your face? Why do you forget our affliction and oppression?

²⁵For our soul is bowed down to the dust; our belly clings to the ground.

²⁶Rise up; come to our help! Redeem us for the sake of your steadfast love!

For Better Or Worse

How is my opinion of God altered in times of great suffering? *"Now there was a day"* ... when Job lost everything (Job 1-2:10); livestock, laborers, real estate, his health and all his children. His wife advised him, *"Curse God and die."* (Job 2:9) I guess she assumed that life wasn't worth living if it meant living with loss.

Job replied to his wife's counsel with a sobering question we would all do well to ask, *"Should we accept only good from God and not adversity?"* (HCSB, Job 2:10)

I have to ask myself, are my acts of obedience currency I dole out to God in exchange for desirable conditions? Do I believe worship obligates Him to do my bidding? Is my love for God contingent upon acceptable circumstances? Or do I love Him simply because He first loved me, and that is unalterably true in the best and worst of times.

_____

_____

_____

_____

_____

Psalm 45

To the choirmaster: according to Lilies. A Maskil of the Sons of Korah; a love song.

¹My heart overflows with a pleasing theme; I address my verses to the king; my tongue is like the pen of a ready scribe.

²You are the most handsome of the sons of men; grace is poured upon your lips; therefore God has blessed you forever.

³Gird your sword on your thigh, O mighty one, in your splendor and majesty!

⁴In your majesty ride out victoriously for the cause of truth and meekness and righteousness; let your right hand teach you awesome deeds!

⁵Your arrows are sharp in the heart of the king's enemies; the peoples fall under you.

⁶Your throne, O God, is forever and ever. The scepter of your kingdom is a scepter of uprightness;

⁷you have loved righteousness and hated wickedness. Therefore God, your God, has anointed you with the oil of gladness beyond your companions;

⁸your robes are all fragrant with myrrh and aloes and cassia. From ivory palaces stringed instruments make you glad;

⁹daughters of kings are among your ladies of honor; at your right hand stands the queen in gold of Ophir.

¹⁰Hear, O daughter, and consider, and incline your ear: forget your people and your father's house,

¹¹and the king will desire your beauty. Since he is your lord, bow to him.

¹²The people of Tyre will seek your favor with gifts, the richest of the people.

¹³All glorious is the princess in her chamber, with robes interwoven with gold.

¹⁴In many-colored robes she is led to the king, with her virgin companions following behind her.

¹⁵With joy and gladness they are led along as they enter the palace of the king.

¹⁶In place of your fathers shall be your sons; you will make them princes in all the earth.

¹⁷I will cause your name to be remembered in all generations; therefore nations will praise you forever and ever.

Glimpse Of Glory

I strive not to make too much or too little of human greatness I encounter.

Though we are finite, frail and flawed in so many ways, God has endowed His image bearers with remarkable abilities that amaze and inspire. It is exhilarating to see people with feet of clay ascend to untold heights.

Still, no degree of achievement erases the guile of the Garden, the curse of death earned by independence.

Our greatness is spectacular, breathtaking, but only a glimpse of true glory, that of our Maker. May the remarkable story of humanity with all its tales of triumph stir our souls and send our gaze heavenward where complete and untarnished majesty truly resides. God is the King of Glory!

_____
_____
_____
_____
_____
_____
_____
_____
_____
_____

Psalm 46

TO THE CHOIRMASTER. OF THE SONS OF KORAH. ACCORDING TO ALAMOTH. A SONG.

¹God is our refuge and strength, a very present help in trouble.
²Therefore we will not fear though the earth gives way, though the mountains be moved into the heart of the sea,
³though its waters roar and foam, though the mountains tremble at its swelling. Selah
⁴There is a river whose streams make glad the city of God, the holy habitation of the Most High.
⁵God is in the midst of her; she shall not be moved; God will help her when morning dawns.
⁶The nations rage, the kingdoms totter; he utters his voice, the earth melts.
⁷The LORD of hosts is with us; the God of Jacob is our fortress. Selah
⁸Come, behold the works of the LORD, how he has brought desolations on the earth.
⁹He makes wars cease to the end of the earth; he breaks the bow and shatters the spear; he burns the chariots with fire.
¹⁰"Be still, and know that I am God. I will be exalted among the nations, I will be exalted in the earth!"
¹¹The LORD of hosts is with us; the God of Jacob is our fortress. Selah

Holding Out Hope

All of creation is in a tantrum (always has been), revolting like an angry child against its consequences of the fall in Eden (see Genesis 3). Natural and un-natural disasters plague our experience and fuel fears of living in a world we cannot control.

What if it all were to crumble? What if our greatest nightmares interrupted our waking hours?

God would still be the great I AM.

We would still find safe refuge for our souls in an all-sufficient Savior.

The redemptive plan of God would carry on unimpeded, certain of fulfillment at the moment He has appointed.

As impossible as it seems, when my world is unraveling ... I can rest assured that God will hold me together. I need only to listen, watch, wait and hope (expectantly) for Him to show. *"Be still and know that He is God."*

_____

_____

_____

_____

_____

_____

_____

_____

_____

Psalm 47

To the choirmaster. A Psalm of the Sons of Korah.

¹Clap your hands, all peoples! Shout to God with loud songs of joy!
²For the LORD, the Most High, is to be feared, a great king over all the earth.
³He subdued peoples under us, and nations under our feet.
⁴He chose our heritage for us, the pride of Jacob whom he loves. Selah
⁵God has gone up with a shout, the LORD with the sound of a trumpet.
⁶Sing praises to God, sing praises! Sing praises to our King, sing praises!
⁷For God is the King of all the earth; sing praises with a psalm!
⁸God reigns over the nations; God sits on his holy throne.
⁹The princes of the peoples gather as the people of the God of Abraham. For the shields of the earth belong to God; he is highly exalted!

Shout!

Arenas come in all shapes and sizes in all parts of the world. Tens of thousands file through their gates to be entertained, paying tribute to their champion. These are the adult playgrounds of our day, grand monuments to their designers ... though few within their walls actually play. Most contribute to the occasion with a raucous roar, shouts of triumph for every step toward victory.

Why is it that we rise so effortlessly, so religiously with raw zeal for human achievement and remain so comparatively composed while extolling our God? Why does the victory achieved on a cross at Golgotha not evoke an eruption of praise in our sanctuaries unlike any heard in a stadium of sport?

How can we be so inhibited in the King of kings' presence while so boisterous in homage to mere mortals?

Could it be that our joy of redemption is mingled with shame over what our transgressions have required of our Savior? Or perhaps we've yet to appreciate the full magnitude of the love so lavished upon us?

Whatever the cause, may the goodness and glory of our God now stir us so completely that our songs of praise would dwarf even the applause of angels. *"Shout to God with loud songs of joy!"*

_____

_____

_____

_____

_____

_____

_____

_____

_____

_____

Psalm 48

A Song. A Psalm of the Sons of Korah.

[1] Great is the LORD and greatly to be praised in the city of our God! His holy mountain,

[2] beautiful in elevation, is the joy of all the earth, Mount Zion, in the far north, the city of the great King.

[3] Within her citadels God has made himself known as a fortress.

[4] For behold, the kings assembled; they came on together.

[5] As soon as they saw it, they were astounded; they were in panic; they took to flight.

[6] Trembling took hold of them there, anguish as of a woman in labor.

[7] By the east wind you shattered the ships of Tarshish.

[8] As we have heard, so have we seen in the city of the LORD of hosts, in the city of our God, which God will establish forever. Selah

[9] We have thought on your steadfast love, O God, in the midst of your temple.

[10] As your name, O God, so your praise reaches to the ends of the earth. Your right hand is filled with righteousness.

[11] Let Mount Zion be glad! Let the daughters of Judah rejoice because of your judgments!

[12] Walk about Zion, go around her, number her towers,

[13] consider well her ramparts, go through her citadels, that you may tell the next generation

[14] that this is God, our God forever and ever. He will guide us forever.

Zion's Zip Code

Alluring destinations of all kinds bid us come; hide away, escape the dreariness or difficulty of life, if only for a moment, and find rest.

For centuries, the people of God found respite and renewal with Him in literal locales. God, of course, is everywhere present; but He chose to "show up" in particular ways and particular places ... a burning bush, a mountaintop, twin pillars of fire and cloud, a wooden chest and eventually a temple in a city (Mount Zion/Jerusalem).

That God would "show up" at all in a broken world full of rebels is astounding; but that He would leave the infinite glory of Heaven, *"take on flesh and dwell among us"* (John 1:14), defies all expectations. And still there's more ... The Creator of all things wasn't content to merely be **WITH** us. He ultimately chose to be **IN** all who would receive Him by grace through faith (John 14:16-17; Ephesians 1:13).

Our greatest place of rest isn't a place, it's a people. There is no more stunning destination on earth than a community of Christ-followers inhabited by the Spirit of God living as the people of God displaying the love of God to the glory of God!

_____

_____

_____

_____

_____

_____

_____

_____

Psalm 49

TO THE CHOIRMASTER. A PSALM OF THE SONS OF KORAH.

¹Hear this, all peoples! Give ear, all inhabitants of the world,
²both low and high, rich and poor together!
³My mouth shall speak wisdom; the meditation of my heart shall be understanding.
⁴I will incline my ear to a proverb; I will solve my riddle to the music of the lyre.
⁵Why should I fear in times of trouble, when the iniquity of those who cheat me surrounds me,
⁶those who trust in their wealth and boast of the abundance of their riches?
⁷Truly no man can ransom another, or give to God the price of his life,
⁸for the ransom of their life is costly and can never suffice,
⁹that he should live on forever and never see the pit.
¹⁰For he sees that even the wise die; the fool and the stupid alike must perish and leave their wealth to others.
¹¹Their graves are their homes forever, their dwelling places to all generations, though they called lands by their own names.
¹²Man in his pomp will not remain; he is like the beasts that perish.
¹³This is the path of those who have foolish confidence; yet after them people approve of their boasts. Selah
¹⁴Like sheep they are appointed for Sheol; death shall be their shepherd, and the upright shall rule over them in the morning. Their form shall be consumed in Sheol, with no place to dwell.
¹⁵But God will ransom my soul from the power of Sheol, for he will receive me. Selah
¹⁶Be not afraid when a man becomes rich, when the glory of his house increases.
¹⁷For when he dies he will carry nothing away; his glory will not go down after him.
¹⁸For though, while he lives, he counts himself blessed —and though you get praise when you do well for yourself—
¹⁹his soul will go to the generation of his fathers, who will never again see light.
²⁰Man in his pomp yet without understanding is like the beasts that perish.

Death's Toll

Worldly acquisition, consumption, expansion, achievement, supremacy, and fame ... woefully temporary attempts at security and significance, none of which alter the harsh reality of Eden's curse.

Death is the price we all must pay for our fall. *"All have sinned and fall short of the glory of God"* (Romans 3:23) ... *"The wages of sin is death"* (Romans 6:23). This death is both physical and spiritual, the second being far more significant – eternal separation from God. No one is so exceptional, so spectacular that their earthly accomplishments even begin to compensate for their spiritual deficit.

Death cannot be outwitted. An attempted bribe is laughable. It is no respecter of person, save One. The One that got away is the One that stole death's sting (1 Corinthians 15:54-57). He defeated death with His own death, burial and resurrection (Romans 6:9-10).

So, while death comes to us all, it doesn't have the last word. Some of us will close our eyes trusting in trinkets to satisfy sin's debt and spend eternity suffering our shortage. But others will breathe their last earthly breath only to take their next in the atmosphere of Heaven having entrusted their debt to the Christ who *gave His life as a ransom for many* (Mark 10:45).

_____

_____

_____

_____

_____

_____

_____

_____

Psalm 50

A PSALM OF ASAPH.

¹The Mighty One, God the LORD, speaks and summons the earth from the rising of the sun to its setting.
²Out of Zion, the perfection of beauty, God shines forth.
³Our God comes; he does not keep silence; before him is a devouring fire, around him a mighty tempest.
⁴He calls to the heavens above and to the earth, that he may judge his people:
⁵"Gather to me my faithful ones, who made a covenant with me by sacrifice!"
⁶The heavens declare his righteousness, for God himself is judge! Selah
⁷"Hear, O my people, and I will speak; O Israel, I will testify against you. I am God, your God.
⁸Not for your sacrifices do I rebuke you; your burnt offerings are continually before me.
⁹I will not accept a bull from your house or goats from your folds.
¹⁰For every beast of the forest is mine, the cattle on a thousand hills.
¹¹I know all the birds of the hills, and all that moves in the field is mine.
¹²"If I were hungry, I would not tell you, for the world and its fullness are mine.
¹³Do I eat the flesh of bulls or drink the blood of goats?
¹⁴Offer to God a sacrifice of thanksgiving, and perform your vows to the Most High,
¹⁵and call upon me in the day of trouble; I will deliver you, and you shall glorify me."
¹⁶But to the wicked God says: "What right have you to recite my statutes or take my covenant on your lips?
¹⁷For you hate discipline, and you cast my words behind you.
¹⁸If you see a thief, you are pleased with him, and you keep company with adulterers.
¹⁹"You give your mouth free rein for evil, and your tongue frames deceit.
²⁰You sit and speak against your brother; you slander your own mother's son.
²¹These things you have done, and I have been silent; you thought that I was one like yourself. But now I rebuke you and lay the charge before you.

²²"Mark this, then, you who forget God, lest I tear you apart, and there be none to deliver!

²³The one who offers thanksgiving as his sacrifice glorifies me; to one who orders his way rightly I will show the salvation of God!"

Accountability

Accountability ... So painful, but so good for us.

We are not autonomous creatures. We have freedom to do as we please, but we are not free to escape the consequences of our choices.

We answer to one another, but most importantly, we answer to a holy God. We are mistaken when we live as if the day will not come when our choices are put to the test, whether they are from a heart of faith or stubborn self-rule (1 Corinthians 3:13-15).

Accountability is ultimately a joy to those who thankfully submit to God's standards and ensure eventual reward (Colossians 3:23-25; Hebrews 11:6). It is an infuriation to those who wish most to have immediate gratification over the great gift of eternal life.

We are at our best when we are willfully dependent upon and responsive to the grace-saturated wisdom of God the Father, lavished on us by His Son, His Spirit and His word.

_____
_____
_____
_____
_____
_____
_____
_____

CONCLUSION

You made it! 50 psalms ... 50 conversations ... 50 intimate steps with your Heavenly Father. I wish I could be right there with you as you cross the finish line of this leg of your journey. Imagine me on my feet, arms in the air, cheering you on with reckless abandon! Way to go!

My heart for you has been that you would encounter the voice of God in His word and engage it honestly with your own thoughts, feelings, questions and intentions. The prayers of the Psalms assure us that we can *confidently draw near to God and find grace to help in time of need.* (Hebrews 4:16)

If you took the step of putting your own words on the pages of this book, then you hold in your hands some of the most valuable material you will ever possess ... God's words and your response. Cherish them and keep them as a reminder of His desire to speak to you through His word. I love how Eugene Peterson describes prayer in his book, *Working the Angles.* "Prayer is not something we think up to get God's attention or enlist His favor. **Prayer is answering speech.** The first word is God's word." Few things in this life will be more precious to you and your legacy than the interplay between you and God.

Having made your way through one third of the Psalms, you can return to these again and again as a reference point and a guide. Not unlike learning a new language, you've been acquiring new words, phrases and concepts. Your expanded jargon will progressively renew your thinking about God and His redemptive activity in your life and throughout the world.

Practically speaking, you are becoming well-versed in spontaneous conversations with God on behalf of yourself and others. As you face life's circumstances, you will have a reservoir to draw from that is full of life-giving and faith-building truth. Your outlook will be shaped by an eternal perspective rather than one bound by temporary conditions. When people around you are in need, you can comfort them with timeless encouragement, the same encouragement you received from your time in the Psalms. The Apostle Paul says it this way, *"Blessed be the God and Father of our Lord Jesus Christ, the Father of mercies and God of all comfort, who comforts us in all our affliction, so that we may be able to comfort those who are in any affliction, with the comfort with which we ourselves are comforted by God."* (2 Corinthians 1:3–4)

Having said that, I hope you will build on the momentum of your experience by applying this approach to other segments of Scripture. What you've done in the Psalms can be done in any part of the Bible. You will encounter other forms/genres of Scripture, but the basic principle is the same ... God speaks, we respond. The Bible is God's voice to humanity and therefore is intended to guide and encourage us in our walk of faith.

Years ago, I learned a helpful process of studying the Bible from Dallas Theological Seminary professor Howard Hendricks that I still practice today ... Observation, Interpretation & Application. I start by thoroughly reading the text, taking note of what it says and how it says it. Then I dig deeper, drawing upon the work of trustworthy interpreters to discover the timeless meaning of the text. Finally, I set out by God's grace to apply what I've learned to the everyday choices of my life. *Note: For extensive help in Bible study methods, pick up a copy of **Living By The Book** by Professor Howard Hendricks.*

The last challenge I want to leave with you is this ... strive to live out your journey of faith in community with others. Make every effort to put yourself in committed, relational environments where you can share what you are learning and glean from others what they are learning in the Scriptures. I believe with all my heart the words of Solomon, *"Two are better than one, because they have a good reward for their toil. For if they fall, one will lift up his fellow. But woe to him who is alone when he falls and has not another to lift him up!"* (Ecclesiastes 4:9–10) Living in community is messy, but authentic relationships are central to God's design.

Thank you for traveling this stretch of the road with me. There's a lot to be said for finishing what you started. It never happens by accident, that's for sure! God graciously uses our simple willingness to show up again and again in His word to lead us to beautiful places. And I can't imagine anything more pleasing to Him than for His children to seek Him. I hope that this venture fuels your desire and determination to pursue the heart of God as a way of life for the rest of your life.

CPSIA information can be obtained at www.ICGtesting.com
Printed in the USA
LVOW07s0854281214

420636LV00002B/347/P